TURN YOUR
PAIN
INTO
ART

ONE SELF-HATER'S JOURNEY TO SELF-LOVE,
AUTHENTICITY, AND CREATIVE FREEDOM

Turn Your Pain Into Art

Copyright © 2018 Ariel Bloomer/Happy Hurts Publishing

ISBN-978-0-692-99565-5

HAPPY HURTS
PUBLISHING CO.

Printed in the United States of America

First Printing, 2018

Turn Your Pain Into Art is available in paperback, audiobook and e-book format.

Visit the author's website at: www.arielbloomer.com

CONTENTS

Like most self-indulgent artists, I've always kept diaries, and by age ten I had amassed dozens of spiral notebooks and bound journals. I thought I was a fascinating little thing, and figured one day the rest of the world would care a great deal about what my favorite color was or what I wanted to be when I grew up. My sister also had me convinced that I could sell all my diaries when I inevitably became famous, and my mother always told me from a young age how important it was to keep all of my writings. "Make sure you hold on to those, Amy!" she'd say. "You'll wish you had them when you get older!" As a result, I grew up fearing that my careful documentations would be burned in a fire, or perhaps become sentient and throw themselves away.

It wasn't until I was about twelve that I took diary-keeping to the next level. By that age, it wasn't cool to call it a diary (what are we, like, nine?) so I advanced to keeping journals instead. I clung to those journals for dear life, knowing that they'd be my future's only connection to my present. They were to serve me for the rest of my life as time travel capsules, and if I did my job right, I would be able to treasure these sacred texts for decades to come.

A few months ago, I pulled my overflowing box of journals out of the closet to set them up on the shelf in my studio. I thought it might be nice to flip through them every once in a while and reflect on what I'd written—perhaps when I needed some inspiration. After organizing my impressive collection neatly on the bookshelf, I pulled out one of my old favorites, which I had titled "My Day Away From the Institute"

1

as a fourteen-year-old, and began to read from random pages.

My heart sank slowly as I took in the familiar scrawl. My breathing grew shallow—every new line just sucked more breath out of my lungs. The air in the room grew increasingly heavy and I lowered myself to the floor under the weight of it. I kept trying to focus on the words, but my head begged my hands to close the notebook.

After a few more minutes of struggling, I had to admit defeat. These journals were possessed; haunted by the mindsets I once thrived on, swimming in the despair that used to be my normal. Like an ex-addict coming into contact with their substance of choice for the first time since getting clean, I realized how easily I could get sucked back in. I took a deep breath, closed the notebook, and packed all my journals back into the box in the closet to gather dust until the next time I gathered courage. I wasn't yet ready to look past me in the eye.

Growing up is hard to do. We all know this. It's ugly, messy stuff, and honestly, I'm still doing it. The process doesn't stop when you reach the magical land of your twenties as I'd always assumed it would. I eagerly await the day when I wake up and find a real, live, functioning adult sleeping in my PJ's, in my bed. I hope she is happy, I hope she is free, and I especially hope that she appreciates all the stuff I am currently working through to secure her a stable place in the grown-up world.

I often fantasize about my future self. I like to picture her floating through the day in a pretty 1920s house with an adorable front porch and constant sunshine streaming through the windows. I am wearing really cool high heels that miraculously don't hurt my feet and my hair is always voluminous and shiny. My kitchen smells like lemons. I have lots of friends and a banging career where everyone loves me, appreciates what I make, and generally believes I'm brilliant and ahead of my time.

I imagine I'll be super busy with my volunteer work and traveling the world and all that, but maybe every once in a while I'll find time to look through my latest box of journals and read what my current self, this girl in her twenties, is presently writing.

I hope my future self is amused by all of this, but has very little in common with me. I hope that by then I will have grown so much that revisiting my current beliefs and mindsets will make her cringe and promptly return the box to the closet. Maybe by then I will do so with fondness, not fear.

In many ways, that's what this book is about. It's about learning to face your past and grow into your future. It's about getting to know yourself—and love yourself—well enough to stop unhealthy cycles and habits that aren't serving you. It's about taking your pain and turning it into something useful, and maybe even one day something beautiful.

PART 1
PAIN

CHAPTER 1

HUSTLING AND HEART SUPPRESSING

I was on a plane, and I was flying.

Flying is straight-up magic, of course, and everybody knows it. You board in one place, in one time, and you come out in a whole new place, a whole new time. And in between, you are…suspended. Simultaneously frozen and speeding through time and space. Floating, flying. Like I said, it's magic.

When I'm on planes, I take special care to take advantage of this magical space. I double-check that my MacBook is fully charged and within arm's reach and that I'm semi-rested and fed, because I find I'm infinitely more creative while flying. My soul tends to serve up a fascinating (to me) cocktail of ideas that I type out like a madwoman in an effort to not lose what I'm certain are the secrets to life being transferred from head to laptop. Sitting thousands of miles above the planet gives me a special vantage point on my own life, and it makes me feel objective enough to make real, valuable commentary on the state of my existence as well as everybody else's.

But during this particular time and in this specific space, the magic of flying wasn't working for me. I was on my way to Amsterdam with my bandmates Shawn, Adam, and Josh. At the time, it was just the four of us traveling to the shows—we couldn't afford a tour manager or a stage tech like the other bands we would be sharing the stage with later that week. Shawn, Adam, and I had started this little rock band, Icon For Hire, four years earlier, and this was only our third overseas gig ever, so it was a big deal for us.

I was sitting at the back of the plane, wedged between my bandmates and a balding, middle-aged guy, trying to conjure up some sort of appropriate emotion to match the novelty of playing an international show. Flying across the Atlantic to play music was kinda cool, right? Shouldn't I be excited? I suspected that I should be feeling something along the lines of *giddy*, but lately all I could focus on was how miserable I felt.

"You're going to Amsterdam!" squealed a little voice in my head.

"I know," I replied dryly (also in my head, in consideration for nearby passengers).

"Your band is playing a big, fancy festival overseas! You're on the main stage! You're living your dream!"

"Yep."

Sigh.

I couldn't evoke the emotion that my peppy head voice assumed should be coming naturally to me in that moment. This had been a bit of a regular problem for me lately. When I say "a bit," I truthfully mean that I'd been having this issue for years, and it was getting worse. The most annoying part was that my life wasn't getting worse—it was actually slowly getting better, which freaked me out, because I was still generally unhappy.

I don't deserve to have this amazing band and these great opportunities because I can't even appreciate them...I'm such a brat...What is wrong with me?...I'm falling into depression again, I know it...Winter is coming...I never properly dealt with all my teenage issues...I can't believe I'm in this band trying to help people get over their crap when I can't even get over mine.. What a joke.

My head continued to serve up more and more of this maddening chatter over the next few hours. I was stuck on a plane, not feeling the magic. Worse than that. I was losing it.

The air wizards must have sensed my distress and finally decided to wave their wands, taking pity on the pathetic girl in aisle 58 having a nervous breakdown. In the midst of my moping, 30,000 feet up in the air, the stream of thoughts stopped long enough for a more helpful, constructive concept to get through.

I.

Hate.

Myself.

Those words hit me hard, an arrow straight to the chest. They cut through the noise and hand delivered a message just for me. I couldn't ignore it, because it felt too much like truth. I had enough lies circulating in my brain that when a thought containing some actual truth presented itself, I couldn't look away. I knew it was dead-on.

Yeah, I *did* totally hate myself. I was actually really awesome at it. It was my secret weapon for keeping myself in line and Getting Shit Done. I didn't really see a problem.

In that moment on the plane, however, it felt like an older, wiser part of my soul was stepping in and saying, "This is not okay! You can't keep treating yourself like this! You don't get to go around all day feeling guilty for your own existence!"

My soul had never said that to me before, so I didn't know. I wasn't conscious of my self-hatred because I was so used to calling it "normal." It was just the air I was used to breathing; I had no idea it was toxic.

That moment where you suddenly see how crazy and screwed up you've let your life get is a big deal. I've had about two and a half of those moments in my lifetime, and all two and a half times my world has changed drastically because of them. Those moments wake us up, and until we wake up, there's no way to know we've been sleeping.

As I sat there staring at my tray table and the top of the guy in front of me's head, it took a minute to all sink in. I considered this newfound "I think I hate myself" thing the rest of the flight, wondering what my next move should be. I chewed on the concept all the way through Dutch Customs, and again as I settled into the hotel bed that afternoon for a jetlag-induced nap.

But I couldn't sleep. The idea wouldn't leave me alone.

I...don't...like...myself.

Weird. Why not?

I don't know! I suck at stuff like this. Why didn't I realize this sooner? I should've fixed this years ago. God, I'm an idiot.

Like myself? Who even "likes" themselves? I "liked myself" in the same vague way that I "liked" freedom of speech or the invention of electricity; it just sort of faded into the background of everyday life. And really, why did it even matter if I liked who I was or not? I obviously had the *confidence* I needed to be seen and heard; I made a living singing my heart out on stage for God's sake. I am pretty sure I was doing just fine. Still, the reality remained.

I figured that what actually mattered was how I behaved externally—my work ethic, my hustle, my day-to-day interactions with others. Who cared what was going on internally? Apparently, not me. As a result, my head was a miserable, cruel place to live in. And until that moment on the plane, I was technically fine with running a hate campaign of one inside my own mind.

Because you know what? It worked.

~~~

People in Amsterdam smoke a lot of weed, and I'm willing to bet that I had a respectable contact high by late Friday night when *she* took the stage.

I had to squeeze in closer to the sweaty crowd to try to take in what was happening on the platform fifty yards away from me. I could have flashed my pass and watched the set from the side stage, but I wanted to experience a show from the audience's viewpoint and get lost in that buzzing feeling of being one with the crowd. Under an open sky, worlds away from home, I was moved in a way that reminded me why I make music. Later that night, I'd journaled about what I experienced:

August 17, 2012

Tonight, a girl went on stage and smiled a big bright smile, and she looked so calm and happy. She had electric energy, and she moved in a fresh way and looked like she was genuinely enjoying herself, like she understood what this moment was. She did not look like she had played the exact same songs the night before. She did not look like she had played to this crowd size and bigger many times before. She looked overcome by her surroundings. She did not give off the vibe that she was vain or spent too much time in front of the mirror, but she was beautiful. Captivating, the star of the stage.

I don't often get swept away by other artists on stage, so when I do it's a pretty special moment for me. I was smitten. Whatever she had, I wanted it. Whatever she had, I would do whatever it took to get it. I knew I would be taking that same stage the next day, and all I could think about was emitting that same energy that she had been emitting so effortlessly. It wasn't even about me wanting to be a captivating *performer*; it was about being a sane, happy *human*, which it really looked like she was pulling off.

When I read back through that journal entry recently, I felt a little sorry for myself. I hadn't ever felt that way about myself. I had to journal it out to process it because I didn't really understand what it was about her that I was so drawn to. As I was writing, I replayed the night in my head, trying to put my finger on what had impacted me so fiercely.

Finally, I realized what it was, and it sent my brain spinning: For the first time that I could remember, I was witnessing someone who didn't look like she hated herself.

If you think that's a little dramatic, you're probably right (I'm a freaking artist, guys. We can usually get away with it.) Regardless of this, I had this very distinct impression that she was *free*. She was playing by different rules from the rest of us caught up in the game—climbing and hustling and heart-suppressing. She seemed happy to be around herself. Like just being her was good enough. She wasn't running, she wasn't avoiding or numbing or doing any of the hundreds of things that I tended to do to get away from my true self. She was just glowing…in her own glow.

To be fair, I never even talked to her. I saw her from several yards away with fancy stage lights and all the other sorcery that a live show entails. So I could be making her all up. Doesn't matter. My soul needed an inspiration, and one appeared. Just like that. I'd take it.

Sometimes, you don't know just how sick you are until a healthy person walks past you and takes your breath away. The combination of the "Surprise! I hate myself!" moment on the plane and the encounter with the girl who looked like she loved herself was cosmic synchronicity at its best. It felt like God showing off a well-timed play. The universe was telling me to get my shit together.

~~~

I'm not one to experience drug-and-God-induced revelations and then just forget about them, so I resolved that the very next day I would focus all my energies into trying to love myself. I woke up early that morning, eager and buzzing, and went down to the lobby for a European continental breakfast. The breakfast room was mostly empty, and I was grateful for the chance to eat by myself and continue processing everything that had happened the night before.

As an obsessive over-analyzer, I never pass up a good chance to sit alone and think through my life. I picked a pretty table near the window and eyed the ducks wandering the sunny courtyard as I artfully arranged fancy cheeses and jams on freshly baked bread (European hotels put America's continental breakfasts to shame).

As I munched, I thought about the strange, scary yet wonderful things I'd been experiencing on this trip, and about what to expect from the day ahead. I had been told that we would be picked up around nine o'clock for a Q & A session on the festival grounds. After a quick magazine interview, it would be time for lunch (food breaks are always a key highlight of my day) followed by radio interviews and filming acoustic performances in the afternoon. Later that day we would play a one-hour set in front of five to seven thousand people, and then wrap up the night with a meet and greet in the merchandise tent.

As I went over the itinerary, I began mentally prepping myself for the day. Big shows like the one we were playing can make me feel a little off until showtime, like I can't quite exhale until the show is behind us. I knew this particular anxiety of mine had the potential to ruin a whole day in a beautiful country, so I began visualizing myself being on stage, owning it, and enjoying it.

I didn't want the day to fly by in a blur of events and new faces, and I decided to experiment—to try a couple of things and see if they could help me slow down and enjoy the day ahead instead of spending it in a state of tense anticipation. I was just certain that my whole life was about to change; that "life starts now" and "today is the first day of the rest of your life" and every other big cliché I could imagine.

Like any good researcher, I over-documented my findings the next day, hoping for the chance to one day share them with you. Well, here they are: Day One of realizing that I kinda hated myself, and that I wanted to change.

August 19, 2012

Day one of loving myself was a smashing…success! YES! All day long yesterday I tried to walk slowly with my head up, to talk in that purposed tone of voice, remain present, and block out thoughts that were wrong. I got frustrated about 30 min before we went on stage because I had so much adrenaline and my body felt nervous.

That was the only time I felt I did not have control. I was worried I would not enjoy the show and my mind would be attacked with panic and all the pressure of the show with the cameras and all that.

But I ENJOYED THE SHOW! This is huge for me! I have not "felt" like that on stage in a long while. I kept remembering, "This is my time, I will take it and enjoy it" and I was present and it was not a burden. I am so excited that we have another show and I get to have my moment of shining again today. This morning I found myself looking forward to the next show...I am surprised that that is rare. I didn't know just how unhealthy my insides had become.

Just to rant, it is incredible what a difference Liking Yourself makes. It is incredible how everyone else can tell me over and over how much they like me—friends, fans, family—and yet that does not make one bit of difference on the inner dialogue. OH one more thing about yesterday—It was late evening and it occurred to me that I was enjoying the whole day! I was not miserable, notably unhappy, waiting to leave. I have found myself so unhappy lately, I was confused, because I know my life is amazing—my home, my man, clothes, body, band, creativity—and I did not know why I was still kind of miserable.

Now as I realize how often I think negative things about my looks, posture, clothes, everything, it makes sense. When I like myself, I like my surroundings. I feel like I've found the secret of life. I will do anything to hold on to this revelation.

Looking back at this, I believe I was right. I *had* found the secret to life. The rest of the tour I continued to play around with these new concepts and ideas. My world was pulsing with possibility, and I felt like *this could change everything*. I had grand visions of flying back to the States and spending a couple more weeks processing everything and then living out the rest of my days in a utopia of self-love, maybe doing some Oprah tours teaching the rest of the world all my tricks.

Um, that did not happen.

What I didn't understand back then was that the journey of moving from self-hate to self-love was just that: a journey. It's been a long one, and some days I feel like I'm more off balance now than I was before I started this whole thing. My path has been messy and complicated—sometimes far more human than I'd like—but the payoff is that I've been learning some really good stuff along the way.

~~~

I've always said I would never get a tattoo*. I thought that I was too unstable and inconsistent to love one thing for long enough to get it inked into my skin, and I knew that the act of immortalizing something on my body would be enough to make me immediately lose interest in it.

However, sometimes I have these brilliant moments of clarity where I understand a concept or a truth that previously has been cloudy and confusing to me. Sometimes I'll get my tea just the right strength and the sunlight will be working its spell on me and it all turns into a glorious, divine revelation where I understand something new and marvelous—something God and the universe have likely been trying to show me for a very long time.

"Understand" isn't what I mean, exactly. I mean *digest*; I *digest* a truth and welcome it as the newest member of my belief system. The others squeeze in to make room, and I shower the new kid with love and praise and attention. I tell all my friends about this new epiphany, and I spend hours journaling on it to make sure I don't lose it. I'm also always so worried about losing it that, in these moments, tattooing the latest revelation across my forehead or something inevitably crosses my mind.

But instead of racing off to the nearest tattoo parlor, I've taken to writing the phrase or quote or revelation on hot-pink Post-it notes instead—which is pretty much just like getting them tattooed, I'm pretty sure. I line them up one by one on the back of my closet door in pretty little rows. I delight in how organized I am, and I hope no one ever sees my Post-it note altar to enlightenment.

No such luck. There was a leak in our apartment while we were on tour over the summer, and the maintenance guys had to come in and rip the carpet out. They moved the entire contents of our three-bedroom apartment into the kitchen because it was the only room that didn't have any water damage. You can bet they got a surprise dose of Ariel's Philosophical Genius™ when they opened my closet doors. You're welcome, Bill and Earl.

In moments of boredom or blankness, I sometimes revisit the closet door of brilliance and read a note, and more times than not I have no idea what I was talking about. It doesn't resonate anymore. Or, perhaps even more strangely, I won't remember writing the note at all and will have no idea why I would find that little snippet relevant. But even if these bits and pieces no longer speak to me, I'm glad to have written them down in the first place, because they were clearly important to me at the time.

Here's where I'm going with this: This self-love thing is so important that we should probably all go get it tattooed across our foreheads—at the very least, maybe Sharpie it there every morning. I promise that this concept is so huge and so life changing that we need to do whatever it takes to soak it up. Post-its, tattoos, reminders on your iPhone, whatever—this is something we need to remind ourselves of every single day, and even if what makes life beautiful and amazing a year or a month or even a day ago makes you cringe now, that doesn't make whatever that revelation was any less important.

Of all the Grand Shit I've discovered in my life, the process of learning to un-hate myself has been the most powerful thing I've stumbled upon. I think it's relevant to share that with you, because I don't want to waste your time. I've read a lot of books that claim to have the magic answer for all of life's problems. I've tried the law of attraction, seven-step programs (it's always seven), you name it—and to be honest, those concepts never really change my life as much as the authors seem to believe they will. I try really hard to get into it, but I usually end up feeling like a loser who doesn't get it but I proceed to finish the book anyways so as not to hurt the author's feelings.

As I've toured the planet, meeting human hearts from all corners of the globe, as I've connected with our listeners via every social platform I can get my hands on, and as I've evolved into someone who cares deeply about the state of our souls, one thing has become clear: People need to know about this self-love stuff. Hating ourselves is a real, persistent issue that unfortunately affects a whole freaking lot of us. Talking about my own self-love journey has been one of the most well-received issues I've addressed with our fans, and people genuinely, consistently resonate with it.

This is simultaneously horrifying and comforting to me. Horrifying because, *oh my God, I am so heartbroken that you feel this way about yourself,* and comforting because *oh my God, thank you, I'm not the only one.*

There is something *really, really* powerful about owning up to our pain. About sharing our stories. The nature of self-hatred is such that anyone who is living in that place is ridiculously hard on themselves and not about to let people in on their twisted thoughts about themselves. But if in a moment of bravery I can gather the strength to hint at the truth—at the fact that so many of us appear to have our lives together on the outside but are in fact suffering terribly inside—that's where freedom is found.

Almost everyone I describe this truth to immediately gets it, but at the same time, this creates so many questions for me. Like, if a whole freaking lot of us are running prison camps of self-hate inside our heads, can we all just stop? Can we take a minute and figure this stuff out together? If we're all just tormenting ourselves with what crazy and ugly and lazy and awful human beings we are, couldn't we all consider dropping it and letting ourselves chill out for a second instead? Maybe catch our collective breath and back off this self-hate thing for a bit?

I'm convinced we can, and I believe many of us within creative communities—whether your creative soul expresses itself in music, painting, design, writing, or even through just enjoying these things from the outside in—are especially craving a few moments of relief.

Traditionally, artists haven't been especially happy people. We're known more for our depressive episodes and suicide attempts than for leading lives of bliss and contentment. There's a reason why "tortured artist" is a thing and "tortured biologist" isn't, but I'm not okay with perpetuating that old stereotype anymore.

I want to be the best artist I can be, yes, but never at the expense of my sanity. And I know now that I don't have to continually suffer for my work. I have enough pent-up pain to pull from for lifetimes of art-making; I don't need to stay in the darkness in order to create meaningful songs and art and a life I feel good about. I have learned to take the pain I've experienced (and continue to experience, since pain is an unavoidable part of being alive) and let it propel me forward. I have learned to forge my suffering into gold.

Admittedly, I don't have a fancy formula for how I do this figured out yet. The specs are still kinda fuzzy. Every morning I wake up with fresh resolve to make today different, better, and I spend my days trying out a concoction of patchwork theories and ideas that have more or less worked for me before. Sometimes it works, but not always. In light of this, my intention here is not to spell out *The Seven Steps to Self-Love* or anything like that. It's more like, *Hey, Do You Hate Yourself, Too? Wanna Swap Stories and Figure This Stuff Out Together? Cool.*

I think it's catchy, but it was too long for a book title.

This I do know for sure: We cannot afford to keep bleeding for our art—or for anything. It doesn't have to be like this. Once I learned to value myself enough to care about how *I* felt about my life instead of just focusing on the final product I was pedaling out to the external world, I realized I could use the pain I had endured to make beautiful things, but I didn't have to stay in that place of pain in order to keep making more beautiful things.

If there's a secret, it's this: learning how to have it both ways. That authentic connection to your temperamental, tempestuous soul *and* actual sanity in your day-to-day life. Your artist's heart and happiness are not at odds, even though it can seem like they are. The most unique and messy parts of you are some of your biggest assets in your journey to joy.

In this book, I've decided to share some of the pain that I've collected in my lifetime, and how I've turned that pain into the greatest artwork of all: a life I am finally at peace with.

*I did end up eventually caving on the tattoos. Never say never, right? I'll tell you all about them later, because all of us folks with tattoos assume the rest of you are extremely interested in our ink.

CHAPTER 2

ROCK AND ROLL FANTASIES

May 5, 2003

I wasn't going to write tonight but this is my way of reminding myself I'm not okay. I wish I could get help. It's so hard, because I don't think I have too much crap, it's not so bad. Is it healthy to tell yourself you're worse than you think you are? I wish I had a therapist. A Christian one, who heard from God. Someone to tell me if I'm normal or not. And then tell me what to do. Because either way I'm unsatisfied. Dude am I expecting too much out of life? WHERE DID MY DRIVE GO?!

Here's how I got started.

I was born on a chilly Swedish night in September to two beaming parents. My mother was due to deliver me any day, and my father had taken her on a walk along the *trädgård* (garden) around their apartment complex to help get labor started.

As a pregnant woman, my mom was a natural—the poster mother for doing things right. She didn't drink or smoke, ate a healthy, all-natural diet, and while she was carrying me she wrote a book about it. A whole book! If I ever get pregnant, I will have big shoes to fill (and a manual written by my mother to tell me how to do it). I have yet to read the whole thing myself, but sometimes when I was little she'd snuggle up on the couch with me and my brother and read us select portions, sparing us the weirder and potentially traumatizing stuff.

My mom was beautiful, as all mothers are. She had long brown hair that cascaded down her back, and she would style it into pigtail braids as all Swedish mamas with long hair should. She had high cheekbones and big eyes, thin lips and a kind smile. She was born and raised in Sweden, and bravely came to America on her own when she was twenty. I never figured out much about her childhood except the bits and pieces I've collected from remarks made by my father throughout the years.

Swedes are traditionally much more reserved than Americans. I've always felt lucky that my mom passed the cool parts of her upbringing on to us, like salt licorice and Jul traditions, but left most of the typical cold Scandinavian demeanor in her past.

Growing up in Sweden was kind of enchanted. The food is delicious, the people are gorgeous, and the gift of experiencing not one but two cultures—not to mention the gift of being bilingual—is not lost on me. Celebrating birthdays was a highlight, where everyone woke the birthday girl or boy with presents and breakfast and chocolates and the rest of the family would sit in their beds as they opened their gifts. Christmas was also extra awesome because we celebrated it on the evening of the 24th, and getting to open presents twelve hours before our American friends was something my siblings and I liked to make a point of at school.

Much of my family still lives overseas, and I miss them in ways I can't describe. Belonging to two different countries also means that you never quite feel all the way home. Wherever you are, your heart is longing for somewhere else—you're missing the other half of your family, and the other half of yourself.

My dad was born in Minnesota in the 1950s, the eldest of five children. He lived through a painful childhood, and seemed to have inherited some deep scars from the father who had raised him. Despite that, my dad was a devoted husband and family man, and always made time for us. He became fluent in Swedish after only six months in the country, and then spent his days getting his PhD at Lund University and his evenings chasing us around the house before tucking us all into bed.

They named me Amy Victoria Ariel Bloomer (and insisted that "Amy" be pronounced the American way, as opposed to the Swedish *Ah-mee*), a name they didn't settle on until three days after I was born. The doctors initially told my parents that I was a boy based on the way the umbilical cord was wrapped around my legs. Having elective gender ultrasounds administered were uncommon in Sweden back then, but even if they'd been popular, I don't know that my parents would have wanted one. My mother was always committed to doing everything as naturally as possible. I imagine her saying, "Ultrasound machines are sketchy! Shouldn't we just trust God with the sex of the baby?"

Twelve hours after I was born, I was introduced to one of my favorite, most influential people in my life: my sister. My parents took special care to let her be one of the first people in the world to see me, covering me up with a blanket so Mercedes would get the first look.

She was ridiculously excited to see me, as she should have been—she practically wished me into the world. If my parents didn't care much either way about my gender, Mercedes certainly did. She wanted a *sister*, a fact she began making abundantly clear to my parents at the persuasive age of three. My parents kept telling her that it was up to God, but that she could pray about it. She jumped in with her whole heart and prayed for me nonstop. Her passion for me even before I was conceived was telling. She spent the third year of her life petitioning for me, and every year of her life after that taking care of me.

Mercedes was a proud older sister. She spoiled me with love and attention, and when she tells me about those early years together she still gets tears in her eyes. She loved me enough for a whole country.

May 18, 2003

Will I ever be okay? When will I be able to stop rambling on? When will I be able to be myself? When will I feel safe enough to stop hiding? In 1,206 days. 1200 days too much.

When I was two years old, my mom and dad came home with another baby, my brother Benjamin. My sister had been telling me how wonderful and fun little siblings are, and our parents revealed him to us in the same way I had been; shielding him in a blanket until we could get the first look. They sat us down on the floor right inside our front door and we held our breaths as we pulled back the covers to reveal a tiny, tight-fisted little boy whom we loved instantly. We took him in as our doll—just like Mercedes had treated me—and took turns fighting over who could hold and dress him. Our family kind of rocked at welcoming babies.

Mercedes took the role of firstborn seriously, and took it upon herself to teach me everything she knew. When I was two years old, she began teaching me dance routines to perform for the family. She would pick a track (usually Swedish pop singer Carola or a children's church song) and coordinate an entire performance, patiently teaching me the steps along the way. She'd dress me up in her beautiful, bright-orange-and-green sequin tutu and sit my parents down in the living room, promising them the performance of a lifetime.

For these performances, Mercedes would introduce me to the audience like only my big sister can, and then cue the track on our tape recorder as I dramatically entered the room, ready to wow my family with the moves I had learned moments earlier. I'd bust out a breathtaking three-and-a-half-minute dance routine, and my sister would pass a cup around the audience, encouraging the crowd to do their part to support the local arts. Mom or Dad would throw in a *krona* or two (about ten cents) while Mercedes would put in her whole allowance. All of our hard work paid off, and we'd be left beaming over the contents of the cup, celebrating a successful performance and dreaming of what we would do with our earnings. She was my first and favorite talent manager.

June 8, 2003

When things go wrong, on goes their music. And now, something is terribly wrong, and I can't listen. The music, that I can handle. But the words... They hurt too much. Every line is like a fucking knife in my deepest core. This. Is. Wrong. They have done so very much for me. I need them. I can't stop my life source! Damned either way though. I'm disgusted with myself.

Dancing in the living room was just one of the dozens of ways that my sister primed me for the real stage. I cannot overstate her influence on me and on my beliefs about myself. When she told me I could do something, I believed her absolutely. My big sister knew everything and was never wrong. I was her protégée, her disciple, and under her leadership I grew up believing that I was a performer, an artist. When she told me that I was destined to be a world-famous superstar, I didn't doubt a word.

While I'm really touched by how deeply she has always believed in me, as a six-year-old kid, she may not have been qualified to declare that I was going to be A Super Famous Singer, and I can't say my own overconfidence in this belief always necessarily served me. When I look back on it now, I'm able to connect a lot of the dots as to why I grew up so darn certain of my impending success—and why I've sometimes been troubled by the general lack of instant, overnight celebrity that I was so sure would be right around the next corner.

June 11, 2001

I want to be a rockstar. Not surprising-who doesn't, but if being real is my base, becoming a rockstar is my hope. I mean, life is crap a lot, and music keeps me alive, it keeps all of us functioning, if you can call living second by second, breath by breath functioning. I just want to be able to give back, you know? I am so very appreciative of the words and beats that have kept me stable each day. The incredible, talented, unselfish people have stepped up and have decided to be my suicide prevention. Where would I be without those beautiful, unreachable heroes?

So, ya, I wanna be a hero, too. I'm sure a part of it is to make me happy and feel like I'm doing something right, good. But I honestly think I just want to have people helped.

Mercedes and I took prepping me for celebrity very seriously. We wrote literally hundreds of songs and spent hours recording them into our super cool cassette player (we *loved* that tape recorder), and sometimes sang the really good ones to our mom to see if she liked them. Moms have to like their kids' songs, you know.

I remember being three years old, crouched on our bedroom floor and singing made-up words into that beloved tape recorder. I don't mean that I made the words up as I went along; I mean that I made up the sounds. I had heard American music by then and knew that everything sounded infinitely cooler in English, but I only knew Swedish at the time. My solution was to just sing made-up sounds and hope it sounded like English. I'd record my gibberish and eagerly listen back, nearly certain that I was singing in perfect English. If only my childhood self could have known that one day I'd get to sing in English as much as my heart desired.

After Ben was born, we moved from the apartment complex to a rented yellow house on a quiet street. A few doors down from us was Mercedes' very cool friend Matilda, and they'd often let me tag along and play with them. I started my first singing group with the two of them. We were called The Champions (note the American name; we were trying to sound edgy), and I obviously didn't actually "start" it at all. I was hand-drafted by Mercedes to be a part of it, and was completely content to obey her every word.

The Champions never went on tour—the world wasn't ready for us—but we did manage a few solid performances around the neighborhood. We'd dress up in our flashiest clothes (arguing over who would wear that fabulous orange-and-green sequin number), grab a tambourine and our hairbrush microphones, and stand in the window while singing our little hearts out. We enjoyed performing, sure, but we weren't just doing this to bless the neighbors with our gift of song. We had a real and pressing motivation behind our performances. We were going to get discovered.

"Getting discovered" is a concept that every young artist is acutely aware of. It lets you skip all the hard years of grinding it out, making a name for yourself, and paying your dues, and allows you to jump straight to the top for no apparent reason other than some big shot declares that you've got the X factor.

And honestly, who doesn't dream of being suddenly swept away by a talent agent in the grocery store who later tells VH1's *Behind the Music*, "I could just tell she had *it!*" Am I right? If this was true for most little kids growing up, it felt a thousand times more true for me. Mercedes had me convinced that my moment of discovery was bound to happen any day now; a notion she earnestly believed in, as well. Standing in that window all dressed up and showing off my mad skills, I was sincerely under the impression that at any moment a black limo would pull up our tiny road. Someone important-looking would step out, announcing that they were "just in the neighborhood, but blown away by the talent coming from your open window."

It took me a few years to realize that it usually doesn't work that way.

If impromptu window concerts didn't get the job done, I was banking that my street performing with our local church would. In a pretty reserved country like Sweden, it was quite a sight to see all the kids in my congregation lined up in downtown Malmö and Göteborg, singing church songs in the town square while our parents would ask to pray for spectators as they walked by. It was a pretty great technique employed by the church we attended: gather a crowd using the cute kids singing in matching t-shirts and then have the parents approach the unsuspecting onlookers in order to share the gospel. Gotcha.

Since my dad worked at the private school associated with the church, we spent a great deal of time there. My siblings and I would show up with our parents for church-building projects, outreach efforts, and weeklong revival services, not to mention attending church, school, and daycare there. For those early years, it felt like our lives revolved around church meetings and outreaches, and since Sweden was (and continues to be) largely areligious, it was easy to immerse ourselves in this strictly Christian church culture that stood out like a beacon. So we did.

June 14, 2003

I look around and despise everything. Myself especially. Even suicide doesn't satisfy.

…I don't deserve to breathe. Not suicidal though, don't worry your precious little head. You try to take the best of me, go away.

I was approaching six years old when my dad announced to the family that we would be moving to the United States. He had been offered a new job in Minnesota, and we were eager to embrace this new opportunity for a couple of reasons. For starters, that church we were so heavily involved in had begun to show signs of becoming a cult (bummer). In addition to this unfortunate church/cult mix-up, my mother was the ultimate adventurer who'd taught us to fully embrace the thrill of new opportunities.

We packed up our whole house—tape recorders and all—and my brave parents flew three young children across the world. When we arrived, we stayed in a temporary apartment and lived out of a few suitcases while a cargo ship carrying all of our belongings took over a month to catch up. We used my aunt's card table as a dining table, and our parents took us to an American grocery store to each pick out our own American breakfast cereal. After ten minutes of nervously pacing the aisle and weighing my options, I settled on my very own box of Lucky Charms. This was quite possibly the most exciting thing that had ever happened to me in my young life.

I was speaking perfect English in a couple of weeks. America would work out just fine.

After enjoying our new home country's variety of pleasures for about a year (the highlights of which included the many sugary, colored breakfast cereals and Barney), we moved to a small town called Excelsior. We rented an old, tiny, white house that my mother loved and my father tolerated. We only lived there for two years, but it was easily one of my favorite parts of childhood, because a single mother with two children, Bobby and Taylor, lived next-door.

If I had to choose one period from my childhood that constituted the word "idyllic," it would be when we lived next to Bobby and Taylor. Mercedes teamed up with Bobby and they began running the neighborhood as respective queen and king of the streets. They converted Bobby's old, run-down (read: falling apart and totally dangerous) garage into the neighborhood clubhouse and ran an elaborate street gang out of it, complete with dues and meticulous attendance records. Bobby was the president, and Mercedes clocked in at a close second with her role as treasurer, carrying a fanny pack weighed down with coins.

I got the part of secretary, which at the time I assumed was a very important job, but looking back now I see they just gave me busywork to keep me out of their way. Taylor was the vice president, and various neighborhood kids filled in other positions as they came and went. Poor Ben got stuck with the role of "guard," a position we tried to convince him was totally noble but really consisted only of standing outside the door keeping watch so that he couldn't play with us inside.

Excelsior was tiny, and the downtown featured a cute restaurant, a small beach, and a movie theater. Bobby and Taylor would attend showings of *Father of the Bride II* while their mom was at work, and they ended up writing the whole script down from memory when they'd get home. We got the bright idea that we could put on a neighborhood play based on their makeshift script and charge all the parents to attend, just like a real play. The next several months were spent in intense, focused rehearsals, though looking back I realize that it was mostly just Bobby and Mercedes practicing their kissing scene over and over again.

The play never made it to the stage, as our family moved before it had a chance. Our new house was a dark-green duplex situated next to a Walgreens and just five minutes from our church. Lots of great things happened in this house, most notably the birth of our little brother.

Over the years, Mercedes had convinced Ben and I that having a baby sibling was the best thing in the world—an experience that I didn't exactly remember and Ben had no way of knowing. We didn't see any hint of a baby on the way, though, so naturally we proceeded to take matters into our own hands. We'd regularly meet up in our rooms with copy paper and crayons and make signs to try to convince our parents to give us a baby—homemade banners featuring big letters with helpful phrases like WE WANT A BABY and HOW ABOUT TWINS? We pulled this trick more than once, often surprising our parents with signs taped up all over the house when they'd come home from a date night.

All that arts and crafts time paid off; when I was ten years old, we finally got the baby we'd so desperately begged for; our little brother

Noah. Noah was, and continues to be, the darling of the family. He's had two parents and three siblings fighting to hold him all his life, but somehow he's managed to grow up into a balanced, kindhearted human being. Looking at him today, you'd have no idea how fiercely we spoiled that kid.

It was also in the green-house period that my dad decided to build us a playhouse. He spent long hours outside, lovingly constructing a masterpiece and occasionally glancing at the instructions we had picked out together from Menards. That playhouse was our hideout, our clubhouse, our sleepover headquarters, and, most importantly, the local police station where we solved neighborhood crime.

Being in such close proximity to the Walgreens gave us an honest look at some of the harsh realities of life. Teenage employees would smoke cigarettes with their friends out back, but we knew there was more to it than that. There was obviously a drug ring, with the older kids using their Walgreens employment status as a cover for the whole operation. We began combing through the dumpster by the parking lot, hoping to find the evidence we needed to call the cops and bust these drug lords once and for all. Unfortunately, we never found the proof we were looking for, but that dumpster boasted a wealth of other wonderful things.

Did you know Walgreens throws their stuff away? At least they did back then.

After a big holiday, they clearanced out all their seasonal stuff, and whatever didn't sell ended up in the dumpster by the parking lot! Can you imagine our joy when we found out? Mercedes and I would throw Ben over the edge and clutch his ankles while he dug through garbage bags and Burger King wrappers to find the loot: fuzzy Easter chickens that walked when you wound them up, Peeps in every color imaginable, baseball cards that we were certain were worth millions, and countless other types of useless crap that we could not believe was just waiting for us to find it.

We'd grab as much as we could carry and then bring our loot back to the playhouse to negotiate over the most coveted items. This went on until our parents started asking where all our new toys were coming from; then they told us that we weren't allowed to steal from the garbage anymore.

~~~

Mercedes and I had a special relationship dynamic; I held on to her every word, and she adored me. With Ben and I, things were different. It took me a few years to go from seeing him as the annoying little brother that our mother made us "include" to the ingenious, wonderful person that he is.

Siblings have a special advantage over the rest of the population where trying to be friends is concerned; they already understand each other in ways that no one else can. Having grown up together, having dug from the same dumpster, having the same belief systems—these things make for an especially unique bond.

One of our favorite ways to spend an afternoon was exploring the timeless questions of the universe. We loved getting lost in spiritual theories, tossing psychological reasonings back and forth. We were elementary school kids getting high off of philosophy—not the textbook kind, but stuff we thought up in our heads.

Ben and I relished the thrill of asking the messy questions, taking turns presenting various made-up concepts to each other, and then analyzing them like only a couple of brilliant kids can. (Yeah, I said "brilliant." I swear I was when my brother and I got together.) We knew how our respective brains worked, having practically memorized each other's neuropathways during the thousands of hours we spent studying and discussing together.

When we were about eight or nine, we began comparing the visual patterns in our brains. We'd sort through the alphabet and review what the color of each letter was, and then argue it out when we couldn't reach the same conclusion. We organized our visual maps of the months of the year and reviewed our reasonings for how and why our mental images were constructed as such. We set up at the kitchen table, drawing out how numbers arranged themselves in our heads and not giving up until the numbers got too high and we ran out of paper.

I would later learn in a high school psychology class that Ben and I had a documented brain condition called synesthesia (actually, I remember my psych textbook describing it as a "brain disease," which pleased us both to no end), but at the time we had no idea that what we were doing was maybe a little unusual. We were figuring ourselves out, together.

June 15, 2003

I put on a happy face. Then I had no more energy, and so I stopped. And everybody hated me for it. And as much as I want to please them, I don't have what it takes to fake again.

I'd pull the trigger but I don't have the strength.

~~~

As you may have guessed by now, I am sharing with you the very brightest and lightest parts of my early childhood. It's tempting to reminisce and focus only on the good things and suppress all of the bad. Even as I look back on these memories, I catch myself thinking, "Oh my gosh, I guess my life was little house on the freaking prairie." And yes, I was so blessed, so lucky—but that is not the whole story.

My childhood narrative would be incomplete without giving some real airtime to the topic of *church*. It was a big part of my life growing up—and I don't mean "big" as in "it was really important to me." I mean that it was a massive, loud, and completely dominating part of my childhood. It took over everything, as my siblings and I assumed that it should back then.

To be forthright with you, today I have a genuine, rapidly grow-ing concern with Christianity. I also still have a huge soft spot for it, and I wrestle with painting it as anything but the answer to all of life's problems as I was taught to believe.

It's just that…I was inside of it, you guys. Way, way deep. I know Christianity inside and out. I know the Christian God inside and out. See, we weren't one of those go-to-church-once-a-week families. We had the keys, literally. We lived there (not literally.) My mom ran the women's group and the infant nursery. My dad tithed ten percent of his income, went to men's retreats, taught in the kids' ministry. My siblings and I served in the nursery, participated in outreach events, ran the slide projector, led worship (in kids' church, youth group, and adult services), did puppet ministry (it's a thing!), performed in Christmas and Easter productions, cleaned the bathrooms, did Sidewalk Sunday School, got the big Sonlight trophies for memo-rizing large chunks of the Bible, participated in dance ministry, went to church camps, retreats, and workshops, attended countless revival services, healing nights, special prophecy meetings, worship confer-ences, went on overseas mission trips, ran the pancake breakfasts to fund said mission trips, and when I was homeschooled for a few years, I served as the church secretary every Wednesday. I answered the phones, folded bulletins, and assisted the kids pastor, Ms. Judy, whom I loved.

I wasn't just a Christian. I was one of *those* Christians.

I loved God. I enjoyed doing a lot of the church stuff. It was fun, and I was glad to participate, but it took me years to realize that a lot of the doctrine and testimonies and teachings that I had absorbed in my youth would only prove to be distractions from God rather than the helpful portals to God that they were intended to be.

While my family was very active in the church and religion was a huge part of my childhood, I have had to learn on my creative journey that staying true to my unique voice is not negotiable. Learning to love ourselves means learning to think for ourselves, and sometimes that can clash with faith. We don't get the luxury of creating from our most honest and authentic hearts if we are living through somebody else's belief systems. Unfortunately, religious institutions often tend to silence differing voices instead of celebrating them, and I was about to discover this first hand.

CHAPTER 3

THE MUSIC IS IN MY BLOOD

I haven't always hated myself. If my childhood memories are anything to go by, there were several observable years of normalcy there—or at least years spent in the absence of self-loathing. This distinction is important.

If I'd been born hating myself, then that's an issue in the code on the manufacturing side of things, and a whole other story. Alternately, if this proclivity towards self-hate happened later in life, then there exists a point of reference that I can go back to and say, "My current reality is foreign to me. It is not my true nature. I can maybe go back to feeling sane one day because I've been there before, when I was seven."

Here's what I do know: I was passionately, undeniably *fucked up* as a teenager. Maybe not as effed up as the average teenager, but my pain was deep, personal, and overwhelming—and it took over everything. But even now as I try to tell my story I feel panicky, like I'm looking around the room for some concrete evidence to offer up as proof.

I was doing heroin by age twelve!
I spent half of my adolescence in the psych ward!
I made local news when I tried to jump off a balcony!

I've got nothing, guys. Nary a diagnosis or prescription to my name. Not once did a doctor, therapist, or even school counselor say "something is not right, and you need help. It's not supposed to be like this." I craved the proof, because otherwise I was probably just making it all up, right? I was probably one of *those* suburban kids who needed to create drama and craved too much attention. Ugh.

I now realize that I *was* in what anyone would consider real distress, but I didn't have anyone to tell me this at the time. I was sad, I was between the ages of 13 and 19, and therefore I was just your typical angsty kid. When I was living it, it felt anything but typical. It felt very, very real. I've lived a solid seven years now in post-adolescence and I still use my teenage years as the measuring stick for what real pain feels like. Whenever I'm sad or distraught or feeling crazy now, I comfort myself by saying, "At least you don't feel like that anymore."

Since I never saw a mental health professional about the development of my self-hatred growing up, I came up with another theory:

It was God's[1] fault.

I think my self-hatred came to me disguised as a kind of spiritual humility, announcing the horrors of my sinful nature and my desperate need for a savior.

I can't be certain, but I think spirituality makes the most sense when it is introduced to someone who has already had a few years of stumbling around in the dark on their own; someone who's ready, who knows they need help. But to teach a kid right off the bat that they are a sinner in need of God's redemptive grace, well—as a kid, you just have to take it at face value and go with it. You have to trust that all the adults know what they're talking about and know what's good for you.

This practice of just blindly believing adults can screw with your head in major ways. You learn to stop asking yourself how you feel about something and start asking the people in charge how you're sup-

---

[1] A word on G-O-D. Just to make it easier, I'll refer to God as a "he." I tend to think that God is so big and magical as to take up the space of both male and female. It can often be really wonderful to picture the more feminine, maternal attributes of God, but just for the sake of picking a pronoun and running with it, we'll call God a he going forward.

posed to feel. If you don't understand something, it's because there's a problem with *you*, not with the idea itself. Before you know it, you've obediently trained yourself not to value your ideas or listen to your feelings, because they just get in the way of what God wants for you.

And I think that's how my self-hatred crept in.

~~~

The music is in my blood.

Sound a little dramatic? I was. My obsession with being a musician that began as a small child kept getting more and more serious as I grew. I became particularly set on becoming a *rockstar* when Linkin Park came on the scene and blew my young mind.

It was never about stardom just for the celebrity of it; I needed to be sure that the art I was making was actually working, and that my songs and my story mattered to people. As I reached my preteen years, this desire to make music—to really connect with an audience—began to take over. It started to get really *intense*.

This desire beat in the center of my chest, like a drum that did not let me rest. It should have been a gift, probably, to know my unique purpose so early in life. *I knew.* I knew it deeply, passionately, all consumingly. I was possessed by the purpose that was pulsing in my body night and day. Not casual songwriting, not "jamming with the guys" for fun. This was serious—I could tell. I had to give everything inside of me to pursue making music and sharing it with the world.

It got to the point where I couldn't stand to watch other people doing what I knew I was born to do. I'd see an inspiring music video or go to a concert and end up running home to my room, collapsing onto my bed, and crying my eyes out, daring God to explain why another artist was living my dream and I wasn't. I felt like I was running out of time, and pretty soon all the spots would be taken and I'd be too late to share the fire that consumed me inside.

Being a teenager is a great time to start differentiating yourself from your parents' beliefs and begin figuring out your own values.

I knew this, because I had been warned about it all my life. I'd sat through the teachings of hundreds of smart religious people (pastors, teachers, the well-meaning congregation members) warning me of the sin that would threaten to take me over as a teenager. I was determined to get through those years with as little mess as possible, because I figured that if I restrained my worldly, carnal lusts, my dream was surely waiting for me on the other side.

I don't know if it was the 24-hour prayer meetings or one of the many prophecies I received growing up, but somewhere along the line I began believing that my chance at ever actually making music was directly connected to my level of "obedience." I genuinely believed that if I messed up by acting like a normal (read: unsaved, unsanctified, sinful, etc.) teenager, God would punish me by giving my grand rockstar calling to someone else—someone purer than me.

The pastors at church kept telling me that I was "set apart," and I believed them; I knew I was special because I could feel that purpose pounding within me nonstop. It was the primary reason God had created me, and I could fuck it all up by sinning. So I didn't. I lived about the squeakiest adolescence possible, but I didn't let that stop me from constantly worrying that I was messing it all up.

When I was eleven years old, I began 7th grade at a new public school, where I met Katie. She loved music, too; maybe not in the same desperate, obsessed-with-being-a-musician way that I did, but she was a focused, passionate fan. She introduced me to Linkin Park, writing poetry, and self-harming. She was a wonderful friend, loyal and devoted, and we were inseparable for the next five years.

Katie grew up in a Lutheran home, but her parents had mellowed out much more than mine. Her mom watched soap operas with swear words in them and her dad sometimes drank beer. I got to sleep over and watch MTV2 music video countdowns until past midnight (and then stay up all night feeling guilty about it). I knew that Katie was just a "sort-of Christian" and probably going to hell, and I knew it was all my fault. I shouldn't be watching secular music videos with her—I should be sharing my faith. I should be a better Christian.

To relieve my guilt I would occasionally invite her to church, and also because it became increasingly apparent that this was the only way we would be allowed to hang out together outside of school.

My parents didn't like Katie. They didn't like any of my friends. They'd tell me they were praying that God would give me more Christian friends and ask, "When was the last time you hung out with Susan?" Susan was the youth pastor's daughter.

I know now why my parents were concerned. I knew why then, too, because they made it a point to let me know at every possible opportunity. They were perplexed by my mood changes and new wardrobe choices. "You used to be so happy when you were a baby!" my dad would tell me. "What happened to my little Amy?" My parents were quick to blame any and all of my rebellious teenage behaviors on Katie's bad influence, but I'm confident that I would have discovered punk clothes, heavy music, and self-harming all on my own if Katie and I hadn't been friends.

I hated upsetting my parents all the same. I knew dishonoring them was upsetting to God, and I knew that if I kept it up he'd blacklist me from rock stardom. Mostly, I really hated letting them down.

For reasons that I still don't understand, my wardrobe choices and withdrawn temperament seemed to genuinely *hurt them*, and I hated feeling responsible for that. If I arrived home a few minutes later than their strict curfew, they let me know how much my behavior hurt their feelings before doling out a strict punishment; one that they'd prayed about beforehand. If I wore too much black in one outfit they'd spend upwards of thirty minutes telling me how deeply my clothing choices grieved them and the Holy Spirit before making me change.

My dad lived through a painful childhood, and he was committed to raising us in a strict Christian manner—presumably to spare us the pain that he'd lived through. Sometimes, the line between God and my dad would blur. Once, my father came into my room one night after I had talked to Katie two minutes past the 9:00 p.m. phone curfew and described in painstaking detail what was wrong with each of my precious friends, wrapping up the lecture with "I've been praying for new friends for you. I wish your friends would stop talking to you and start hating you."

I burst into tears. So did he.

A few months later, at a Christian conference, my dad told me that God had spoken to him and revealed that I'd had a curse put on me in my mother's womb; a "spirit of unbelonging." He said it had surfaced when I started wearing chokers. So he collected all the chokers, spiked jewelry, and chains from my room and confiscated them. I got them back some years later when he stumbled onto them right around my 22nd birthday. I still have the paper bag full of my treasured teenage jewelry collection, but I'm not sure why.

Not much later after the "spirit of unbelonging" incident, my father came into my room one day to tell me that he had been praying and felt that I had a "spirit of Jezebel" on me. This freaked me out because my friends and I had recently started a little club called The Jezebelz, and we were wearing homemade bracelets bearing those words. I had hidden mine in a desk drawer so my parents wouldn't find it. I promptly retrieved it and handed it over to my dad, scared out of my mind about what God would tell him next.

I didn't have to wait long to find out. The following week I was sleeping over at my friend Jane's house. We were watching *Sid and Nancy* and slashing up clothes into punk couture in her basement. Our evening was cut short when we heard pounding on the door around 12:30 a.m. It was my dad. God had said I shouldn't hang out with Jane.

My mom heard from God, too. Many times I came home from school to a lecture about how disappointed in me she was. She'd be walking by my room and the Spirit would tell her that something wasn't quite right. He'd then lead her to the teenage beauty magazine/ the non-Christian CD/the PG-13 movie hidden under the bed/in the drawer/on the closet shelf. I was grieving the Holy Ghost, she told me, and that stuff didn't belong in our home. This happened so many times you'd think I would have started stashing my stuff at friends' houses, but I was pretty freaked out by how perceptive my mom was. She'd probably find them there, too—or God would.

The hardest, most painful time "God" intervened in my childhood was when he took my music away.

I was fourteen. My parents came back from a church service and announced that they would be going through Mercedes' and my music collections and getting rid of anything ungodly. This seemed strange to us simply because we didn't really own any ungodly music—the rare non-Christian CD had been long confiscated by then, and we knew better than to have that stuff in the house. So what did they mean?

We found out soon enough. "Ungodly" meant anything with a weird cover and anything resembling rock music. All of our precious albums, collectible vinyl, limited editions—all snatched up to be disposed of. They told us they buried them in the backyard. We wept.

Maybe some could say that having our music taken away doesn't seem like that big of a deal, but it did something to me. It felt like a confusing, cruel move on God's part to alienate us even more from our friends and from our chosen culture—not to mention from the actual music—by not allowing us to listen to bands simply because of their genre or album art. We weren't trying to enjoy the likes of Disturbed or System of a Down; we were listening to straight up "Christian" bands whose CDs we'd purchased from the Christian bookstore and been introduced to by the Christian magazines we read. It didn't make logical sense that God would tell my parents that we couldn't listen to music just because it was heavy, but I was scared to question my parents' ability to hear from God because that would be rebelling.

Besides, if they'd gotten this wrong, then what else could they have misinterpreted?

My parents loved me. They loved me deeply. They protected me fiercely. They did all they knew how to do to create a safe space for me to grow up in. I was a unique kid and they didn't know what to do with me. My black clothes and chains didn't end up getting me hooked on drugs, but they didn't know that. My craving for heavy music didn't end up leading me to worship Satan, but they didn't know that, either. They were constantly worried about me because I was clearly miserable. I didn't have the language to tell them that a lot of their behavior was contributing to my pain, and I would have gotten in trouble for trying to explain that, anyway.

Nowadays, I have a good relationship with both my mom and my dad, and that's something I am so grateful for. We don't talk about the past much, but they've apologized to me for the things they did to hurt me. I wouldn't even have remembered many of the aforementioned events save for my journal entries during those years. At the time, I thought I was able to separate the acts of my parents and my view of God, but upon re-reading the entries now I see how easily one affected the other.

Looking back, I see page upon page of self-hate.

My journals are filled with self-loathing, self-disgust, and on top of that, there was the guilt. I was horrified with myself for thinking so much about...myself. I was pissed at myself for acting like the typical depressed teenager. *I'm better than this, I'm smarter than this,* I thought. *I know better than to feel this way.*

I was a self-perpetuating cycle of judgment and self-hatred. I kept a running mental list of everything that was wrong with me, of anything that might disqualify me from being a Christ-follower and, consequently, from living my dream. I was in turmoil over having gay friends since it went against my church's doctrine. I was terrified that listening to and enjoying mainstream music was sealing my fate in hell. I didn't even consider asking myself how I personally felt about things like mainstream music or homosexuality; I just wanted to "please God." All I could hear was the voice of my parents and the people at church repeatedly telling me that I was set apart, and I took this to mean that I had no right to be a normal teenager.

I drank in the same convincing rhetoric over and over:

Rebellion is as the sin of witchcraft.

Disobedience is demonic.

You are the only Bible some people will ever read. Your actions may be the difference between them going to heaven or hell.

Jesus is coming back any day, will you be ready? Are you really saved? Are you totally sure? You will know beyond a doubt in your heart, as the Spirit will speak to you.

Have you been falling away from the Lord? Have you been living in rebellion? Repent from your sinful ways! The devil has had his hands on you, but you can return into the kingdom.

In retrospect, I recognize this rhetoric as well meant but misguided. I should not have spent my adolescence in a tight ball of nerves, worried that God was going to tell the pastor or my parents that I sometimes listened to rock radio.

~~~

A few months into high school, I found myself with a real, live group of friends. For those of you who perhaps never went to high school or have forgotten, having a group of your own is a pretty freaking big deal. It can take care of a host of issues for you (loneliness, depression, suicidal thoughts), while simultaneously contributing to a host of issues for you (loneliness, depression, suicidal thoughts).

It wasn't exactly that I had found this pack of close, tight-knit friends who would see me through all the ups and downs of my high school career; it was more like I stumbled into a built-in community of freaks who were kind enough to take me in.

I had homeschooled for most of 7th and 8th grade after begging my parents to pull me out of my junior high, and they had kindly obliged. I've always had a difficult time with school, so I was especially grateful to bow out of the notoriously tormenting middle school years. But by 9th grade I was eager to give high school a shot, mostly because Katie would be there, too, and I craved the freedom that leaving my suffocating home environment would afford me.

The summer before heading off to my first day of 9th grade, I made a very intentional, calculated decision. I straight up decided to become a punk kid.

From where I stand, there is really no graceful way to suddenly transition from "normal" to "punk." (The terminology changes every couple of years but the implication remains the same.) My whole life I'd gladly worn hand-me-downs, but as I started to fall in love with heavier music (with or without my parents' blessing), dressing in a way that fit the music started to come naturally to me. I began spending my babysitting money at the local thrift stores and my dad taught me a few basic stitches on his mother's antique sewing machine. I became totally hooked on self-expression and started wearing clothes that made me feel unique, with a handmade style that no one could copy.

I headed off to the first day of high school in a homemade punk tank top, thrifted black skirt, and super awesome used combat boots that were two sizes too big that I wore every day anyway because they were just so freaking great. I also donned Halloween black lipstick, every piece of jewelry I owned, and a backpack I had spent hours customizing with lyrics, patches, fabric scraps, and safety pins. Like all self-sufficient 9th graders, I changed out of my mom-approved outfit and did my makeup every day on the bus on the way to school (and erased all traces of it on the ride home).

That's how I got my free group of friends. All the other freaks saw a new potential member and welcomed me into the existing group with open arms. I don't know how I got to be so lucky, but because of my new homemade style—and because Katie was already plugged into the group—I had instant friends. To this day, it blows my mind that the high school clique system is so predictable, so efficient, and that all I had to do was show up in black for the other freaks to take me in. God bless their little black hearts.

Fans sometimes ask me how I get the courage to dress the way that I do. I think they're expecting a dramatic story about how I just decided to rebel against society and be myself no matter what, but in truth, I haven't had to sacrifice very much over how I dress. If anything, I find it has opened doors for new relationships and conversations, not limited me. Sure, I've experienced real resistance from various authority figures, but that can all be tolerated if you feel acceptance and love from the people who really matter: your friends.

I am so deeply grateful for the safety and sanity that having friends in high school afforded me. The luxury of having a partner to team up with in science class or sit next to at lunchtime was not lost on me. It felt like I had hit the social jackpot just by having people to hang out with.

Of course, just because I had friends didn't mean I was allowed to actually hang out with them. I'm sure it goes without saying that my parents didn't approve of any of the kids I was befriending, and my friends quickly learned to take off their spiked jewelry or turn their Korn shirt inside out before meeting them.

In 10th grade, my friends Katie, Sarah, and sometimes Nikki started a band. We called ourselves Mea Culpa (which means "through my fault" in Latin—how appropriate for a guilt-ridden young Christian punk), until we found out there already was a metal band with that name in Germany or something. We got together on a few odd weekends and tried to write hit songs detailing our deep assortment of feelings. We'd rehearse the same riff for hours and talk about how we needed to get our act together so that one day we could play an actual live show. We didn't make it.

I learned a lot in those first two years of high school. I learned that all my friends had terrible home lives and were generally living in their own personal hells. I learned that if you were bullied or clinically depressed or gay, you got to get out of class and go to special meetings. I learned that the worst story wins. We took solace in each other, sharing our experiences and offering up any comforting words we could think of. Trading war stories and comparing battle scars became a regular part of our morning routine, and we lived for those sacred minutes before the bell rang.

We were all miserable, my friends and I—and I suppose that's to be expected...right? After all, we were the proud token freaks of the school. The kids with shitty home lives and unstable brain chemistry. The ones with weird punk hair and freakish loyalty to our favorite dead musicians.

In fact, it all kind of went together:

The obsession with music.

The misfit clothing.

The intense depression.

It was all a packaged deal. And the better you got at all of them, the more legit you were.

Being authentic was no small thing for us. We liked to throw around the word "poser" a lot. This was the worst thing you could be called. Bailey was a poser because she liked Avril Lavigne. Tego was a poser because he had money, but still wore ripped-up clothes to look cool. Alicia was a poser because on average she seemed pretty happy, and that left us all confused. I just went ahead and started calling myself a poser so no one else could do it for me.

It was never said out loud, but the more screwed up you were, the more legit and the cooler you were. Everybody in my group was bisexual. Everybody cut. Most of the chicks had eating disorders. Stints at the psych ward were cool. Going to therapy for your depression, suicide attempts, running away—these were all pretty legit things.

Sometimes Skyla took the lead with her horrible realities of living with an alcoholic mother.

Sometimes Amber won because she kept getting harassed for being Wiccan and a lesbian.

Sometimes I was at the front of the pack because my parents were crazy oppressive and a thousand times stricter than anyone else's.

All of us hated ourselves, our parental units, and our lives. It was what bonded us together—it felt like our survival depended on it. Without our pain, without our stories, we didn't have anything left. Our entire individual and collective identity was based upon our self-hatred. My friends, my music, my self-expression: they all revolved around my feelings of worthlessness and self-loathing. The pain wholeheartedly defined me, and I was wholeheartedly okay with that.

Of course, any difficult time can be endured when you know it will end. Katie and I began counting down the days left until our 18th birthdays in each journal entry. Seeing *1,231…1,230…1,229…* at the top of the page is pretty depressing in itself, but it gave us something to hope for. We could not wait for the day when we would finally turn 18 and get the hell out of here.

The self-hatred leaked out, as it usually does, in various forms of self-mutilation.

Though I abstained from the drugs and sexual experimentation that my friends (and almost every other high-schooler) indulged in, I managed to get hooked on self-harming. It seemed like the safest option of all the typical teenage coping mechanisms, and I knew I could keep it somewhat private. Since the Bible said nothing directly about self-harming, I hoped that maybe it didn't count as sinning and that therefore God couldn't mark it against me.

I hesitate to go any deeper in sharing my old thought processes regarding self-mutilation. I've never been sure of how to talk about it in a constructive way, and I don't want to glamorize it. Sometimes, growing up, I would hear testimonials from other people who had overcome a certain addiction. Sometimes it was inspiring, but I often found that other people's stories only served to help me to go deeper down that road by unintentionally teaching me their various methods or how they avoided getting caught. So, while I won't describe all the details of how I got into it, I do want to share with you how I got out of it.

~~~

Right before my sixteenth birthday, my dad suddenly moved my family from Minneapolis, Minnesota to the bustling metropolis of Decatur, Illinois. Never heard of it? Me neither. I knew I was in trouble when we drove into town to check it out for the first time and the welcome sign stated, "Decatur: We Like It Here!" Really? Your city sucks so bad you have to defend the fact that you actually enjoy living here? Shit, shit, shit.

I was pissed that we were moving. I had finally found a group of people I could call my friends, and was in no position to move 500 miles away from them. During the eight-hour drive down, I looked out the window at the cornfields and cursed my parents for finding another way to ruin my life. I tried to be hopeful that the new town would be okay. I also decided that now would be a good time to start going by my middle name, Ariel, instead of my first name. There was a band by the name of Evanescence (maybe you've heard of them?) that was quickly gaining popularity, and their singer's name was Amy Lee; obviously, there couldn't be two Amy's on the scene. I also really liked the idea of signing my future autographs as "REL," which would save me countless hours and hand cramps from not having to write out the *a* or the *i* and serve to inform fans that my name was not pronounced exactly like the little mermaid's.

Yeah, it was a long drive.

My dad's company put us up in the town's fanciest hotel, a Holiday Inn on the outskirts of town. I cried myself to sleep for 15 straight nights and tried to make sure that my little brothers couldn't hear me. The more we explored this new town, the more anxious and desperate I became. The first time we visited Wal-Mart I burst into tears yet again at the sight of the sloppily dressed townsfolk in line to buy Crocs and fried chicken. The same thing happened at Krekel's, a local greasy burger joint. I knew very clearly that this was a town I did not belong in, and I would, in fact, not "like it here."

I started school a few months later and was taken aback by the smallness of it, the whiteness of it. Unlike my last school, I did not get free friends because of how I looked, as there were no other freaks there to speak of. Everyone pretty much wore polo shirts and brand name jeans. For the most part, everyone seemed at least mildly happy. I had no idea what to do with that.

My personality simply *didn't work* in a town like Decatur. I was loud and obnoxious, boasting bright pink hair and homemade clothes. I only made sense in the context of lots of other noise and color, which Minneapolis had had plenty of. Decatur was so blah, so yuck, that I realized very quickly that it looked like I was trying way too hard. I liked trying, I enjoyed expressing myself, but in a town like this all you had to do was part your hair to the side and you were instantly emo. I was, simply put, too much.

But as much as I hated that town, I can't deny that moving there did chill me out a bit. As I look back, I realize that it was kind of the start of my personal journey to recovery. I attribute this to a couple of things.

First, being removed from all my friends gave me some space to really think for myself. I loved my crazy friends, but it took being away from them to see how unhealthy that dynamic really was. Being around all these relatively happy peers provided a stark contrast to what I was used to, and it began occurring to me just how miserable I was. Being miserable sucks, but I didn't even know that. I didn't have an objective take on "miserable" until I got some breathing room between myself and my sad friends. For the first time, the part of me that wanted to get well started growing stronger than the part of me that wanted to stay sick.

Second, the town was so small that everybody knew everybody. This bothered me to no end. I love the feeling of getting lost in a crowd (and standing out from the crowd), and there was no real way to do that in Decatur.

A lot of people who went to our new church also went to my new school. I didn't want to be a poser, obviously, so I started to feel a responsibility to at least try to be somewhat…consistent. I was leading worship at youth group, and I thought it might be a good idea to kind of act like a Christian at school as well. Which meant:

1. be nice to people instead of being a withdrawn angry punk kid,

2. don't pretend to be a lesbian with your best friend for shock value, and most importantly,

3. be careful of what the other kids at school hear you say or see you do in case it gets back to your parents because your town is so freaking small.

It forced me to clean up my act.

Ah, and the loneliness. That, too. I spent a lot of time alone in my room, staring at the fields outside my window, talking to God. We developed a special closeness that we hadn't had before. I got some distance from the crazy expectations of the people at my old church and started to feel that maybe God kinda liked me instead of just tolerated me. I felt like I had some breathing room to choose for myself the kind of person I wanted to be.

I realized I wanted to be happy.

I had no idea where to start. But suddenly, in a town like Decatur,

I started to play around with the idea that it would be all right to be happy, because none of my friendships were riding on my suffering anymore. There were no other misfits to confide in about my mental instabilities or self-loathing issues, so I stopped obsessing over them. Before I knew it, I was able to go whole days without feeling that bottomless pit of sadness that had been normal to me for many years. It was a slow process, for sure, and it by no means made me a happy, productive member of society (whatever that means), but it did provide me with some courage to begin climbing out of the dark hole I had grown to know and, if I was being honest with myself, love.

One day, it occurred to me that self-harming was a temporary coping technique, not a practical life skill for long-term happiness. You can't cut forever. You can't be a mother of two in your thirties excusing yourself with a smile to the bathroom to break out your blade because your toddler won't clean up his toys. You can't be a famous singer playing summer festivals and take the stage in a tank top and shorts with fresh cuts running up your arms or thighs. I finally realized that self-mutilation was not a part of my picture for the future, and that I wanted to find better ways to handle my pain. Once I realized these things, a wonderful thing happened; I came to understand that if I stopped creating so much room for my pain, it would stop screaming at me so loudly.

Here's what I know now: Cutting is a symptom; a painfully common expression of the disease that is self-hatred. Just to cover all my bases, let me say for the record that it's not cool, it's not hardcore, and if there is any part of you that is doing it to impress your friends, cash in on the shock factor, gain sympathy, get attention from parents/teachers/therapists, whatever—*stop*. Stop for someone you love. Stop for me. Stop for your future family. Stop for future you. Even if you're an especially "pure" cutter and are doing it for all the "right" reasons or in all the "right" ways (and those are...?), I would also like to encourage you to stop.

I realize this is a bold request on my part. I am aware that it's probably none of my business how you choose to express your pain or exert control or whatever benefit it is that you're getting from self-harming. But as someone who deeply loves you, as someone who has spent much of her life making music and podcasts and writing books for *you*, I'd like to ask you anyway.

So, darling, if you self-harm, please stop. When you do this to yourself, you are flirting with suicide, and that's a powerful invitation of self-hatred into your life. When you make sacred space for mental and emotional anguish, you essentially make it feel welcome by inviting the pain to take off its jacket and stay awhile.

You *can* stop. You *can* heal, slowly, one minute at a time.

Since you are already creating a sacred space for your pain, I'd like to invite you to get in the habit of doing that in a different way. Make a list of alternative practices that you can partake in the next time you get the craving to hurt yourself. Draw on your body. Journal it out. Go walking or swimming or hell, punch a pillow. Call a trusted friend who can talk you through your feelings. Kiss your wrists. Light a candle, put on some new music, and dance around your room to celebrate the freedom on its way to you. The simple act of creating a moment of diversion can be enough to confuse your cravings and let some light in.

Just start where you can. Decide ahead of the pain what you will do the next time you feel the need to harm. When you feel weak, pause to feel my love and all the love in the universe that is available to you. There's freedom on the other side of your pain. You are amazing, and brilliant, and powerful, and I want you to feel that way. I want you to inspire the world, scars and all.

~~~

I survived my two years living in Decatur by making friends with cute boys and by locking myself in my room to play piano.

That piano's keyboard became my safe place where I was free to explore my feelings and not be punished for them. Self-harming, listening to dark music—those were dangerous, but how could God (or my parents) scold me for playing minor chord after minor chord?

I learned how to use fancy recording software and wrote a lot of angsty songs. I started coming down (or more accurately coming up) from the fog of depression that had enveloped me for so long and began learning how to live my life more on my own terms. This didn't mean I was legitimately happy; I just wasn't constantly sad anymore. I assumed that not cutting and not being ultra-depressed was about as good as it got in life. I was fine with that.

Somewhere along the way I had picked up this idea that I had until I turned eighteen to get my whole life together. After that, I'd be a real adult and, most importantly, I could start my band and become a real musician. With my self-imposed deadline growing closer every day, I felt myself growing and changing personally, and I wanted to consider my audience—my fans—and how I could be useful to them. How I could help them. I wanted my listeners to *get it*, to understand what it's like to feel isolated or depressed or crazy.

I also knew I couldn't just leave them there. Because that would be cruel, right?

I thought, *I've got to figure this stuff out so I can go and give them the gift of my story*. It felt like more was riding on my recovery journey than just how it would affect me; like maybe a whole community of people was waiting to see how I would turn out. And it mattered. If I didn't end up okay, I wouldn't know how to help anyone else end up okay, either.

I began to use my fans as my motivation to continue learning, trying, and hoping. I didn't yet have enough self-love stored up to heal for myself alone, but I loved *them* enough to give it my best shot. They were counting on me.

In reality, obviously, there was no "them."

I wasn't in a band and I had nobody waiting to see where my journey would take me, but that was irrelevant, because I knew that one day, my story would matter a great deal to my listeners. I took advantage of my blind belief in my impending success and let my passion help me heal so that I could maybe help others do the same one day through my music.

I know it sounds a little crazy—getting better to help a fanbase that didn't even exist yet. But it actually worked for me. And I invite you to try this: If you don't yet love yourself enough to get better for *you*, maybe you can do it for *them*. Even if you don't know who "them" is yet. It can be your future fanbase, your future followers, your family, your friends, your world.

I believe that people are counting on your recovery. People who could benefit profoundly from your unique story. But you likely won't have the courage, strength, or opportunity to share it if it takes all your energy just to get out of bed every morning.

The world will never hear you sing if you are too scared to write your song.

We will never enjoy your art if you're too depressed to make it.

You will never take the stage if you're knee-deep in untreated anxiety.

You can't show them how to love themselves if you hate yourself.

You won't fulfill your life's purpose if you kill yourself first.

Do you see what I'm saying? Your story matters. Your healing matters. You need to get better for you, yes, but also for all those people out there counting on you. You have big things to do with your life! We need what you have! Please don't hold out on us.

CHAPTER 4

DEMONS AND DRUGS

When I was 17, I traded in the sophisticated charm of Decatur, Illinois for the hot, oversized city of Dallas, Texas. My mother beamed as she handed me the manila envelope from the school I'd been accepted to, CFNI, which stood for—wait for it—Christ For the Nations Institute. This was the very same college at which my parents had first met over two decades ago.

If we acted like it was a big deal, we shouldn't have. The requirements for getting in came down to if you had the money to go (a nominal $600 a month), and if God didn't tell the school not to accept you. I also had to correctly answer a bunch of very uncomfortable personal questions on my application; ones I dared not lie on in case God might tell the school that not only had I smoked pot that one time, but that I had lied about it, too. I couldn't begin my college career by lying to God. After all, I was attending this school for the sole purpose of finally finding him.

I had first become interested in CFNI after seeing their worship DVDs, which featured students getting lost in the music together, smiling, and dancing as they worshiped their Creator. As I had spent many years frantically searching for God, this school seemed like a prime spot to finally pin him down.

I thought God hid from humanity in a cosmic game of hide and seek, and it was our life's purpose to seek him out until we found him. If we could not find him, it was because:

A. You're a hot mess ("there is sin in your life")

B. You're doing it wrong ("you are not seeking him enough/with a pure enough heart")

C. God has a plan ("he doesn't want you to find him at this time, but don't question his will because he knows best")

I suspected that my problem was probably B.

Nowadays, I no longer believe that God hides. I think God is everywhere: in my living room, in the bird singing outside my window, in my piano playing, in my very soul. These days God and I don't fuss much with elaborate games of hide and seek—we generally have free access to each other and get to hang out whenever we want. But back then at 17, I had yet to figure all of this out.

In the years leading up to the college decision, I had grown increasingly fascinated by the booming 24-hour prayer movement, where brave young souls would sing their hearts out round the clock. Literally, they prayed like 12 hours a day and then handed the baton (microphone) to someone else to pray for the next 12 hours. I wasn't spiritual and disciplined enough to pray for 12 hours straight, but it wasn't from lack of trying. I did the Christian equivalent of rain dances in my bedroom, doing whatever I could think of to call God down from heaven. I figured this crazy Christian college would be the perfect place to finally renounce my sinful ways and get God's attention once and for all.

The moment I arrived, I realized that things were weird. On my first day, the staff told me that they *loved* my pink hair, but unfortunately, it was decidedly *not* allowed in the student handbook. After reluctantly dying it black, I headed up to the dining hall, where a good-looking guy immediately approached me. His blue eyes and chiseled jawline did nothing for me, however, the minute he opened his mouth. He followed up "Hey, I'm John" with, "Do you want to have sex?" I did not.

I received my room assignments the next day and was paired with a girl named Marcy, along with Sarah, a sweet freshman who kept to herself, and Nikki, a feisty southerner who ended up getting pregnant (and consequently kicked out) later that year.

My first night in the new dorm, Marcy sat me down on the filthy 70s couch to give me a speech she'd probably been practicing all summer. She told me that this college was "a hospital for sick people, full of broken and hurting souls who couldn't get in anywhere else. I can't be friends with them because that would be casting my pearls to swine." Hello! She thought she was giving me an orientation, but it ended up being a bitch fest during which she called out everyone currently attending on being worldly hypocrites. A hypocrite is the Christian equivalent of "poser," and is the worst thing you can possibly be.

She was a sophomore—and on the official campus worship team, no less—and a psychotic, selfish control freak, bless her warped little heart. She told me as soon as she met me that she thought I was "creepy" and made it a point to regularly drop condescending comments about what I was wearing. I think she was afraid that I would infect her with my weirdness.

A few weeks in I worked up the courage to personalize the dorm to make it feel more like a home. The second she saw my changes she threw a fit and insisted I take it all down and throw everything away. I guess my homemade artwork and Rage Against the Machine posters were not her style.

A few days after my home decorating fail, Marcy announced during breakfast that she and some of the other sophomores were praying for me in their morning prayer circle. She said I had woken up screaming in the middle of the night (which I did not remember, but in her defense, I do that all the time now, so it was probably true), and the girls responded by "interceding" to break off the evil spirits that were holding me captive. How sweet. Marcy had been suspecting I was demon-possessed, and this screaming-in-the-night incident was clear confirmation. Great. First I've got the spirit of Jezebel on me, and now an outright demon's possessing my soul.

I got this kind of stuff from Christians *all the time.* I may have only been 17, but I was well versed in the art of humoring the kind soul that was "concerned for my salvation." I was often singled out at conferences and prayer meetings, where people would come up to lay hands on me and pray the evil spirits off of me. "The demon of oppression is broken! The spirit of isolation is gone!" I'd smile politely and thank them for the free exorcism and let them believe they'd done me a huge favor.

It didn't stop with the churchgoers; worship leaders at large events would step down from the platform in mid-song to approach me in the audience. They'd pray and weep bitterly as they "felt the abuse of my past" or something like that. Although they were clearly mishearing whatever God was trying to tell them, I played along and was usually gracious enough to not call them out on it. I should've let churches hire me out for special services; the little goth girl who will politely get saved and have her demons of rebellion cast out for the hundredth time in front of an audience.

I was, and continue to be, in awe of the lack of awareness among religious circles that self-expression and spirituality can in fact coexist brilliantly. Whenever someone would come up to me after a church service and say, "It's so cool that people like you love God!", I'd be reminded how far humanity has to go. I mean…really, now? You think that the way I dress has anything to do with my relationship with my creator?

God, like me, is an artist. I imagine he has spent billions of hours over the course of humanity designing his babies, complete with blueprints for what their bodies and personalities will grow into. I wonder if his design process is anything like mine, where some days it comes easy and he's on a roll, and other days he gets frustrated and keeps reworking his designs and revisiting the drawing board.

It should go without saying that God loves it when his creations express themselves. I mean really, when we express ourselves, we're actually just expressing God. So we get to dye our hair every color of the rainbow and ink up and pierce up our skin and wear whatever makes us feel most connected to our true selves. We get to show up to spiritual services in our most beautiful display of self-expression, because otherwise we'd be coming before God and our fellow humans dressed up in dishonesty.

But the college I went to didn't know any of this yet.

CFNI had devoted over half the student handbook to dress code specifics, and much of it centered on eliminating self-expression. I was constantly being sent home from class for wearing my handmade clothes that the school deemed "distracting." They encouraged me to refer to the student handbook to review their definition of *Long-Sleeve Blouse* and *Dress Slacks*.

This place was full of all sorts of strange rules. We couldn't walk on the grass. We couldn't have any piercings or exposed tattoos. We couldn't be alone with the opposite sex, and dating was out of the question (but if you were engaged, you were allowed to hold hands off campus, so that was pretty sweet). We couldn't watch movies in our dorms, so people would lie in their doorways with their laptops just outside the door. This was for PG movies, mind you, as PG-13 and R were explicitly not allowed.

No secular music. No Internet access. We were 18-year-old prisoners, threatened with expulsion (and let's not forget hellfire!) if we couldn't meticulously memorize and follow the student handbook. The message was that we had to be pure vessels—a holy generation set aside for the Lord and all that.

While the rules created their own special kind of hell, it was the weird, manipulative nature of the staff that really set off my time at CFNI.

As Marcy started getting more and more difficult to live with, my roommates and I decided to try and switch rooms. We went to the dean to voice our complaint about Marcy's behavior, as she had started snooping in our stuff and going through our text messages. The dean asked us to describe the trouble, and we all took turns sharing our experiences.

"Have you confronted her about getting into your phone?" he asked after we'd detailed our complaints.

"No, I just found out," I proceeded cautiously. "She is…emotional…and I didn't want to stir anything up if I can just switch rooms."

At that, he threw his shoulders back and continued with confidence. "It says in the Bible to share your complaints with one another and *then* bring it to the elders. Since you didn't talk to her first, you're certainly not allowed to switch rooms."

I was back in the dean's office multiple times that year despite my best efforts. They called me in one day and asked me point blank if I was a drug dealer, as some students had seen my friends and I huddled up and passing around a pill bottle. I guess ibuprofen looks like illegal narcotics if that's what you're determined to see. A few months later they summoned me again, this time asking if I was a lesbian. I had held hands with my friend Jess while crossing the street.

~~~

It wasn't all bad, however. It was during my first year at CFNI that I met Tyson, Blake, Jess, Josh, and Brandon. I cannot describe to you how much these people meant to me, but I still want to try.

We met slowly, one at a time, as we picked each other out from among the lifeless, vanilla student body. As much as the school tried to stifle self-expression, we were easily able to locate and identify each other. We were punk kids trying to look like proper preppy saints, but we weren't really fooling anyone.

I met Brandon first. I was immediately drawn to his beach bum persona, tousled blond hair, and mischievous smile. We had tea together in the commons room, which was as close as a guy and a girl could get before raising eyebrows and concerns.

After our tea date (which was not a date), Brandon took me to an abandoned part of the campus where we had a thrilling time sneaking past electrical fences and old concrete ruins, exploring this Texas jungle just outside our campus. We weren't supposed to be there—we were walking on the grass, for heaven's sake! I felt like a little kid lost in Narnia, safe but free. It was a wonderful feeling that I would get to experience several times with my friends over the next nine months.

Josh was easy to spot. He had somehow managed to get the dark red streaks in his spiked hair approved by the men's dean (who was apparently *much* more lenient than mine), and his eyes, set in a round baby face, said that he'd been through a lot for his age. At only 16, he was too young for college, but he had homeschooled and gotten in anyway. He also had a guitar.

To say that I was attracted to guys who could play instruments was a complete understatement. I would cling to them for dear life like my ticket to rock stardom depended on it. Josh couldn't exactly *play* yet, but his vampire-blood-red electric guitar (complete with an amp!) was gorgeous. I was instantly hooked.

Next was Blake. Blake wore band tees outside of class—boys had to wear collared button-ups in class—and never combed his hair. He played drums. He had (and still has) one of the sweetest hearts I'd ever encountered. His precious family took us all in for mashed potatoes and turkey on Thanksgiving since we were all too far away and broke to visit our own families. He still comes to Icon shows and helps load in gear when we swing by Texas. Josh, too; it's always a great little family reunion.

I met Tyson next. He played drums as well, and had come to the college with Jess. They were both from some tiny town in either North or South Dakota, I forget which, where they did things like ride horses and shovel snow. They were a packaged deal, and I couldn't have been luckier to get to be friends with both of them.

And then there were six of us. Making not one but five amazing friends at the same time felt like winning the friendship lottery again, only it was different this time. The memories we made that year were like something out of a movie. I belonged. I belonged. *I belonged.*

Belonging is—dare I say it—everything. It should not be confused with fitting in, which is something else entirely. Fitting in begs to be a part of a social circle, and it is eager to bend and mold in order to qualify. But when you belong, you qualify just because you're you. When you're with a group of people who warmly make room for your soul with no questions asked, stay there. You will know when you've found it because you won't feel like you have to constantly compete for the title of Best Sob Story or Craziest Home Life or Most Legit Music Collection—you'll just fit, and that's it.

The fact that we were all musicians just made it that much better. Tyson and Blake would spend hours arguing over the complexities of their favorite albums and use their forks to bang out drumbeats on the trays in the cafeteria. Brandon played acoustic guitar and wrote love songs for Jess, and Josh was learning to play his guitar at an increasingly impressive rate. You can imagine how the music freak in me was exploding—these were my people! I bugged them nonstop about starting a band and picking a name and getting our first real show together. I was bursting at the seams.

A month into the school year, CFNI announced a talent show, and any student was welcome to participate. This was our chance to finally get a proper rehearsal space, and suddenly we had access to a practice room with a drum kit and a PA sound system! With less than a week to get it together, we began writing a song to perform at the show. Tyson played drums (as Blake hovered nearby making suggestions), Brandon played bass, Josh was on lead guitar, and he enlisted his sister Faith to play rhythm guitar. I was on vocals, front and center, right where I wanted to be. It felt like my lifelong dream was finally coming true.

We talked about nothing else during the days leading up to the show. I skipped class to sew my outfit for the performance, and we practiced coordinated head bangs in the lunch line. The masterpiece of a song that we had come up with in a week was called "Where Did You Go?", and it began with me on piano on the side of the stage, which allowed me to dramatically make my way to the center as the epic chorus hit. Eat your heart out, Amy Lee.

The performance was magical, with only a few minor hiccups. We took third place and first in the Crowd Response category. We were told we would have placed higher, but the panel of judges (a few deans with nothing better to do on a Saturday night) were unsure if all of the lyrics were "biblical." You can't make this stuff up.

If I assumed our debut show would be our ticket to stardom, I was wrong, of course. After the talent show, we lost our practice space and things went back to normal. Josh and I attempted to construct songs on his computer using GarageBand, but since guys and girls were never allowed to be alone together we had to record my vocals in the common student areas. It didn't exactly work out great.

Thankfully, I soon stumbled into the school's network of tiny, secret piano practice rooms—spaces that would come to host some of my most precious musical moments. As a freshman, I wasn't actually allowed to use them, but nobody monitored them so I went for it. The rooms all smelled like musty basements and old people, and were no bigger than a few square feet—enough to hold a piano, a bench, and one person. I'd lock myself in those catacomb-like rooms for hours and bang my soul out on the piano when I was supposed to be studying. I'd write rock songs and pretend that I was playing to an actual audience.

My group of friends turned what would otherwise have been just a painful and lonely year into memories I'll treasure for the rest of my life. We kept watch for each other while one of us slept through the lecture, we stood up for each other, we broke the rules together.

On restless nights and weekends, we would all pile into Tyson's 1998 Chevy van (which we named the Contraband Van, since it was where we all stashed our mainstream albums, movies, and magazines) and make the ten-minute drive into the city, where we would stay out past the school's ridiculous 1 a.m. curfew and dream about our futures. We went to coffee shops and indie shows and walked around empty streets after the city had shut down. When I wrote Slow Down's "Take me all the places that we used to go / the starlit city / our makeshift home," it was the six of us wandering Dallas that I had in mind.

One night, we got so tired of the crazy campus rules that we committed our most rebellious crime yet and stayed in the city all night. We found ourselves stranded downtown at two in the morning, and we knew that if we went back to our dorms then we'd all get written up. So we found a run-down motel in a shady part of the city and pooled our money to get a room.

Sleeping in the same room, much less the same bed, with boys was so scary and so forbidden that I kept waking up in the middle of the night, terrified that God had told the deans what we were doing and that they'd come to drag us back. Thankfully, God kept his mouth shut, and when we woke up in the same clothes we'd slept in and commenced to eat brunch like the family that we were, we all felt accomplished, tight knit, and deeply loved.

Speaking of love, Jess and Brandon fell in it, hard and fast. They came back from Christmas break to announce they had gotten married. We were all happy for them. We found out later they were making the marriage up. They wanted to spend the night together, and faking a marriage was the only way to do that.

I see now that almost every single rule the school made up was to prevent the one thing that every college student wants to have: sex. The ban against chicks wearing tank tops or shorts (this was Texas for God's sake!), the early curfews and ultra-watchful deans, the no-dating policy; these were all put in place to keep us from getting naked and getting it on. All my life, Christian authority figures were practically obsessed with keeping our teenage bodies "pure" until we were delivered to our soulmates, where we would surely enjoy this enthralling experience about which we were allowed to know nothing now.

Now that I've had some time to process this, I realize that having sex before marriage is in no way the tragedy that youth camp described. People who have sex before marriage can go on to lead wonderful, healthy lives full of great relationships. People who save themselves for marriage do not always go on to have incredible, banging sex with their spouses and get divorce immunity from God Almighty. If I could give one piece of advice on this topic, it would be this: for heaven's and your sanity's sake, *never* get married *just* to have sex without feeling guilty. Regretting a night in the bedroom is much less painful than regretting a day at the altar. Come on, now.

A theme that the universe keeps conspiring to teach me is to not judge either way. So whatever your personal convictions are, it's cool, and you don't have to make it your mission to convince everyone to feel the same way about it as you do. Something as intimate as *intimacy* should probably be a personal decision—one we make for ourselves and let other people make for themselves. That way, we can all be at peace with our own respective journeys rather than judging other people by our personal value systems.

After putting up with Marcy for a whole semester, it was finally time to get new room assignments and—praise Jesus!—Jess's room had an opening. I suddenly went from living in a crazy, unhealthy, and dirty environment to moving into a clean, beautiful room that housed not only Jess but her lovely roommate, Whitney, as well. Whitney was only 19 to our 18, but we called her Mom and she spoiled us like her kids, stocking up on dish detergent and toilet paper and fixing us blueberry waffles almost every morning. It was a welcome, wonderful change from the toxic situation I'd grown used to.

Jess and I became especially close; sharing a 400-square-foot living space with two other girls will do that to ya. We would stay up late drinking tea, playing piano side by side, and sharing our secret fears. She told me how worried she was about her alcoholic brother, and I confessed how much I hated praying all the time but that I needed to find God and didn't know what else to do.

Jess was good for me because she was nothing but love and acceptance (the perfect climate to foster belonging, if you recall), but she was also a lot more liberal with her choices. While we both hated the claustrophobic nature of the school, she was the only one who did something about it. After voicing her complaints to the staff, she announced that she was dropping out. My first thought was, "What? You can't do that! What about your parents? What about your life path and all that?" She didn't care. She went and got herself an apartment 20 minutes away that we grew to love and affectionately call The Flat at Jess's insistence. We painted murals on her walls while the boys played their guitars, and during spring break she had us all over for an elaborate Easter dinner.

I wish I'd worried less and had more fun during my time at CFNI. I was trying really hard to be a good little student and a good little Christian, but I eventually realized that even if I slept through class or failed tests or broke their beloved student handbook guidelines, none of these things were pushing me further away from God. I tried so hard to be respectful and to get the approval of the staff, but that was just a waste of time. I've since learned that just because someone is older or is in charge, it doesn't make them right.

Sometimes I daydream about going back to that school knowing what I know now and causing all sorts of trouble. I'd stay out past 1 a.m. and wear tank tops, and I'd invite the other students to fabulous parties. We'd play mainstream rock music and dance. *On the grass.*

After nine months of crazy Christian college, I was a spiritual basket case and I desperately missed my previous life filled with self-expression, even if said self-expression had come with some less-than-savory self-hate habits. But at CFNI, I had been accused of being a drug dealer, demon-possessed, and a lesbian (the horror!) all in my freshman year. In truth, all this rigorous sin-tallying turned out to be the perfect environment for self-hatred. Passionately, directly, intensely. When you hold yourself to impossible standards, you fail. So, yeah, I'd managed to stop physically punishing myself for that, but it didn't mean that I was any nicer to myself than before.

I felt like I'd grown in so many ways but was still stuck in the same old cycle of self-hate as before—just with different scenery (and, thankfully, a healthier social group). Despite the positive things that had happened to me during my freshman year at college, I *was* still pretty miserable, and growing increasingly frustrated with myself for feeling that way. Now that I was 18, an actual adult, it was time to grow up already and stop all my poor-me whining. I'd come a long way from feeling constantly depressed, but I was in no way healthy. And, like always, the only place I could really be honest was in my journals. I'd allow myself to rant about my feelings, but I'd always be sure to tie up my entry with how stupid and selfish I was for feeling that way.

I still had a long way to go.

CHAPTER 5

ICON FOR HIRE

At the end of my year at CFNI, my mother lured me back to Decatur with the promise of laundry room access and regular meals. I had been living below the poverty level in Dallas, and the idea of free food and clean clothes was too good to resist.

I had plans to stay at my parents' house for a week or so and then head off to my next life adventure, whatever that held. Jess had offered me a room in The Flat and I was considering heading back to Dallas to work and spend the summer with her.

I arrived back in Decatur on a Monday, and two days later, I met someone.

It was a Wednesday evening. I was so grateful to have my freedom of self-expression back, and I dressed up in the bottom half of a slashed-up wedding dress coupled with a homemade Linkin Park corset and headed to the Edge, a weekly youth group/hangout that most of the town's 12-to-18-year-olds frequented. I was sitting at a table catching up with a friend when he mentioned that the Edge's band had a couple new musicians.

"There's this new guy on guitar. He just got out of rehab and stuff, and he's helping out in the band. But anyway, he's really good. Oh—that's him coming in now."

I looked up to where my friend was pointing. There in the doorway was one of the prettiest people I'd ever seen.

And he played guitar.

Sign me up.

I approached him a few minutes later and introduced myself. He told me later he could barely understand what I was saying (I'm a fast talker, and even more so when I'm excited) and it came out sounding something like "HimynameisArielandIhearyouplayguitarandwillyouteachmebecauseIreallywannalearn?"

Smooth, huh? I didn't really want to learn guitar, you know. I just needed an excuse to get him alone and convince him to start a band with me.

The next day, I was driving to see my ex-boyfriend for the first time since I had left for Dallas. We had stayed good friends over the year, and I think he wanted to talk me into giving it another shot. I was a block away from his place when my phone rang. The call was from a number I didn't recognize.

"Hello?"

"Hey, Ariel? This is Shawn Jump."

Hot guitar guy! He had called a dozen people trying to track down my number and had finally succeeded. He asked if I wanted to come over and give those guitar lessons a shot.

Sure did.

Standing up my ex that night turned out to be one of the better choices I've made, even though it wasn't very polite of me. I arrived at Shawn's bachelor pad to find he had a freaking *studio*. In his house! Within ten minutes, we were writing together. An hour later, we had our first sloppy scratch demo, complete with guitar and vocals and angsty lyrics. Our chemistry was instant and intense.

Shawn was 23 years old to my 18, so we were gonna keep it strictly business. Everybody knows dating is the death of a lot of good bands, and it just makes stuff way too complicated. Oh, and there was no way in hell I was gonna be the lead singer who is dating the guitar player. Does it get any more cliché? I was not about to be that melodramatic couple that almost breaks up the band when we split up six months later.

Over the next few weeks, I was at Shawn's house every minute possible. He was working third shift at a welding factory, so I'd be over at his place from early afternoon until midnight when he headed off to work. We dug through the hundreds of songs I had written in my lifetime and started taking them from lyrical ideas to full-blown pieces of their own. We bought and borrowed recording equipment and pieced together more rough demos to capture our ideas. We argued over rhythm patterns and song structures. We ate frozen pizza and drank pineapple juice and fantasized about playing a real show one day.

We were, as you probably guessed, fooling only ourselves. All you had to do was walk by us to sense the chemistry between us. People did, and made sure to let us know we were idiots for not being together. In a town of ninety thousand people, we would show up to community gatherings and parties together and people would go out of their way to tell us what a killer couple we made. We were quick to correct them; this was all about the music for us. We were focused and not going to let romance get in the way of that.

This lasted for exactly one month. Not bad, huh? After four weeks of nonstop working on music, we gave in and spent a lot more time "working on music."

It was also around this time that we realized a two-piece band was gonna make for a sparse live show in our local hardcore scene. We needed a drummer. Shawn knew a guy. They used to be good friends back when Shawn would throw huge house parties. This guy would crash at Shawn's place, and they grew to be pretty close after a couple of months. They used to jam together in their friend's garage, banging out Tool and Pantera riffs while their drunk friends egged them on. He also lived just a few houses down from Shawn.

"Perfect!" I said. "Let's invite him over!"

It wasn't that easy. Remember that rehab stint my friend had mentioned? Shawn had done that in an attempt to give up his party lifestyle, and it worked. He'd cut ties with his old friends, and that was how he'd managed to stay sober for the last six months. He wasn't about to jeopardize that by letting this hardcore partier join our band, but after a few more unproductive writing sessions, we thought we'd give party drummer dude a try.

Adam came over and set up his giant drum kit in the dining room. Shawn turned his amp way up, and minutes later we found ourselves in the middle of our first actual band rehearsal. I had a mic plugged into a tiny speaker, and couldn't hear a word I sang over the noise. No matter. The second we started playing together, it was on.

You guys. I was singing with a guitar player *and* a drummer. Who both knew how to play. We were set up in the kitchen and playing our hearts out, and we sounded like a real band. It took all I had not to break into tears. This was the feeling I had waited my whole life for. It clicked. We decided to give it a go.

That was July, and we played our first show in November. There was a nearby venue called Wake The Dead on Eldorado Street that booked local hardcore bands and small national headliners. The place was dirty and held maybe 300 kids. We got the gig by selling a couple hundred tickets.

It blows my mind that we were able to sell over 200 tickets to our first show, and to this day I think we flat-out cheated. Local venues don't usually love booking brand-new bands because they have no idea if you're any good or can actually draw a crowd, but by making the venue a couple grand in ticket sales before the show even started, the venue lost all risk involved and we got to open for a local band that already had a following.

Here's why I say we cheated: The only reason we were able to sell that many tickets was because Shawn and Adam had such reputations as partiers that they knew every freaking person in that town, and they hustled tickets to their moms and their coworkers and ex-girlfriends and all their party buddies. Essentially, people were expecting a good time because they knew that Shawn and Adam could be trusted to make it a memorable night.

We packed the grimy, dark venue on a cold November evening and eagerly took the stage to play our thirty-minute, six-song set. We'd paid an old classmate of mine thirty bucks to play bass, and we were ready to rock. We were anxious to impress what felt like the entire town that had showed up in support, and we wanted to prove to ourselves that we had what it took. I'd been practicing my stage moves and "How we feeling tonight?!" lines in my bedroom for half a decade, so I felt pretty ready to go.

Our set list was a mashup of old songs from Shawn and Adam's jam days that I had written new lyrics for coupled with new songs we had written from scratch over the last few months. We had an epic, drawn-out intro, awkwardly long song transitions, and two-minute breakdowns after every chorus.

Nailed it.

I felt overwhelmingly at home on stage that night. I felt like I was up there doing my life's work. It was messy and emotional and spiritual all at once. It felt like something so much more than just a band playing songs on a stage—it was electric, it made my soul explode. It was like something bigger than me was triggered when I was performing, and this would prove to happen during almost every subsequent show. My heart, my very center, was plugging into the hearts standing before me, my audience. That deep, larger-than-life love I'd felt for my audience since I was little wasn't imaginary anymore. There were real people listening to me sing, and I wanted so badly to impact them in some small way.

We have played over a thousand shows since then, and every single time I'm up on stage, my agenda is still to *connect*. To open up my arms and let my heart bleed out for my audience to see, and for them to connect their hearts with mine. I am not up there thinking, "I better hit this next note" or "I hope all this head banging isn't ruining my hair." I am locking in on the people standing in front of me, the souls who are there with us, watching as a spiritual transaction of sorts takes place before our eyes. It's rewarding and emotionally exhausting, but as the singer and front person, I feel and take this responsibility of connection seriously.

When I'm on stage, I'm not just selflessly giving; I'm taking something, too. I'm leaving filled up, drunk on human connection, and I crave this interaction immensely when we're not on the road. After a month off from playing shows, I find myself stuck online watching old sets of ours, and I often miss those moments so much that I start crying, my heart on fire with the memory of it.

~~~

The band grew. It was beautiful to be a part of, and oh my God, it took *for-freaking-ever*. As you might have guessed, I suspected that now that I was in a Real Live Band, worldwide success was right around the corner. I had lived my whole life believing I'd be launched to the top any minute now, and I was certain that *now* had finally arrived.

Our first show proved lucrative, and we were invited back. A few of the older, more established bands heard about us (and the fact that we could sell tickets) and let us open for them. Within a few months, we were driving to places farther and farther away from Decatur; places like Champaign and Springfield, Illinois, which pretty much meant we were on tour. We usually squeezed into Shawn's Chevy truck, filled from floor to ceiling with all our guitars and drum gear, and took turns on who would pay for gas. In those days, playing shows would cost *us* money, and we worked day jobs to finance our music habit. Who am I kidding—we *still* work day jobs to finance our music habit.

We did whatever we could think of to gain momentum. Since we didn't really know any better, any idea that popped in our heads was fair game. We got online and became well versed in every musical platform ever, spending days setting up band profiles on every social site we could find. We needed pictures, obviously, and some blurry live shots from our first show weren't cutting it, so we paid a kid fifty bucks to take some "professional shots" in front of an edgy brick wall. I began hand sewing and painting shirts I'd picked up at the local thrift store with our band name—Icon For Hire—to sell at our shows, and used the money from the sales to invest in our first run of professionally printed shirts.

We got together with our friend Mike, who had a big, fancy house and high-end recording gear and who was nice enough to let us use it. We tried our best to learn how to work ProTools and mic our instruments, and we recorded our first high-quality demos in Mike's big living room. (Well…"high quality" is a stretch. Maybe more like "we-did-our-best quality." You can look up our song "Sno" online to get the idea.) Mike also let us use his dining room table as the band's Central Operating Headquarters, which is where we set up our laptops and drank coffee and talked strategy as we trolled other bands' MySpace and Pure Volume pages to see where they were playing and tried to jump on their shows.

We cold-called what felt like three hundred venues in the Midwest area and got maybe ten shows out of the deal. We emailed college radio stations fancy pitches about why we belonged on their rotation. We spent hours manually requesting MySpace friends so it would look like we were more popular than we were, and played our own YouTube videos on repeat to get the view counts up.

Our DIY demos weren't cutting it, so we saved up for a few months and went into a real studio with a real producer and made a three-track EP for $1,800. It featured "Off With Her Head," "Pernilla (a.k.a. Only A Memory)," and "Call Me Alive," which hardcore fans still request at shows sometimes.

We wanted to have a big show for our EP release, so we asked the Edge if they'd let us use their venue. They were down. Actually, everyone there was immensely helpful, letting us use their space to practice in and their printers to make fliers for our shows. They believed in us and gave us a lot of the support we needed in those early years.

Our EP release party was exactly one year after our first show, and we managed to get 500 people to pay ten bucks each to get in. We hired some local openers, recruited our friends to run our merch table (including Sarah from the Mea Culpa glory days), and it ended up being an amazing night. We had a two-hour signing line after our set. We sorta felt like rockstars.

That was how we grew, one fan at a time. And even though we were doing well at our hometown shows, we played hundreds of shows for under a dozen people. Sometimes we played for just the venue promoter and the sound guy. Those nights were rough, and made us wonder if what we were doing was making any difference. Still, we could tell we were connecting with the kids who *did* come out to our set, and we could see that what we were doing resonated with people.

We played anywhere they would take us. Birthday concerts in driveways, century-old theaters, youth centers, county fairs, grungy church basements, warehouse clubs, hole-in-the-wall bars; we were in. We played a local Halloween festival that featured "midget wrestling." We played a biker expo at the prestigious McCormick Center in Chicago, where Adam almost got in the middle of a bloody fist fight taking place backstage as girls in bikinis (wearing numbers so the men could vote on who was hottest—the drunk guys next to me kept hollering "get on up there, babe!" at me) pranced around on stage.

We saved up and bought a used 15-passenger van for a few grand, and a kind soul named Kent gave us a trailer to use for our gear. We felt super legit pulling up to shows in that getup. We usually slept in it, fighting over blankets and setting our phone alarms every hour to turn the heat on for a few minutes, but if we sold enough t-shirts, we sometimes got to sleep in hotels.

The first hotels we slept in consisted of Motel 6's and Red Roof Inns, which, if you've never stayed there, just—well, don't. We could only afford one room for the four or six of us, depending on if any friends were along for the ride that weekend. We had to get creative. One of the boys would walk up to the front desk and book a room while we made sure that the staff couldn't see our van and trailer in the parking lot from their vantage point. Shawn or Adam would then go find the room and tell us where to pull the van around so we could sneak in the back way. We were a strange sight, hauling pillows and sleeping bags in from the van at three a.m., smelling of stale cigarette smoke and sweat from the show we'd just played. After a few hours of sleep, we would take turns hitting the breakfast lobby and grabbing bananas and coffees two at a time before getting back on the road.

We also stayed at strangers' houses a lot. There were many times when we pulled up to a strange house in a strange neighborhood in the early hours of the morning and some guy would come out in his sweats to tell us where to park the van. We'd all be very quiet and try not to wake the wife and kids, hauling all those sleeping bags in and setting up on the living room floor and couch to try to get a few hours of sleep. Sometimes we'd wake up to the sight of their little kids poking at us or to the smell of breakfast being cooked. Most of the strangers were very kind, and I am very grateful for their trusting hospitality. A few of the strangers were creepy, and their houses smelled of dog crap or didn't have heat. It was always a fun surprise to see what we were gonna get.

After we'd been at it for a couple of years, we got an email from a record label guy. He seemed legit, so we decided to meet up with him. He bought us lunch and made us feel important. His label was pretty slick and was connected to an even bigger, slicker label, but all his other artists were contemporary Christian musicians, and we could tell it wasn't for us. We hated passing on something as cool as a record deal, but knew our band didn't make sense at that kind of label.

It was right after that when we received a MySpace message from another label guy. Apparently, all that friend requesting hadn't gone unnoticed. This dude was an A&R guy from a label called Tooth & Nail. I showed it to Shawn and Adam—they had never heard of T&N—but we were still excited that they were interested in us.

Over the next few months, we performed showcases and had endless conference calls with this label. We spent a lot of time on the phone discussing the vision we had for ourselves, making sure they understood what we were going for. We (well, I) had concerns, because a lot of their other artists seemed to be kinda Christian, as well—getting Christian radio play and being sold in smaller Christian book stores and the like. We told our A&R guy that we weren't going that route, and he said it was not a problem as the label did mainstream stuff, as well. They would make sure to concentrate on that side of things.

Cool. We signed the deal.

~~~

During this whole grow-the-band thing, Shawn and I remained close, as well. After two years, he proposed on the top of a roller coaster, and I cried and said yes. We got married a year later.

Our relationship and our band began at the exact same moment: the second we locked eyes that Wednesday evening. Since everything we did involved the band, we tried our best to keep some parts of our personal life out of it. Our relationship was untraditional—our dates consisted of playing shows together instead of going to the movies or out to dinner—and it was important to have some part of our story feel safe from other people's input and gazes. We gave so much of ourselves to our band and our audience, and it was healthy to have little things that, for once, involved just the two of us.

That first month that we met each other, we informed people we weren't a couple—and we honestly weren't—so we just kind of kept rolling with that. We didn't lie about it, but we never made a big deal about it. I honestly figured most of the fans knew anyway, like they could see it in the way we looked at each other, but were gracious enough not to ask about it.

The August following all those contracts—our record deal and our marriage certificate—we headed to Nashville to record our first album.

I hated Nashville. We had been there a few times before to co-write with other writers; writing dates our label had set up for us. Our label insisted that *half* the songs on our first album be written with somebody else. I learned quickly that I also hated co-writing. We'd walk into a room with a stranger—usually a nice but clueless flannel-shirt-wearing dude in his thirties—and I'd be expected to pour my heart out and collaborate with this guy. We wrote with five different people and came up with ten songs, and most of them sucked.

I'm not saying the co-writers themselves were awful; more that the experiences made my skin crawl. It felt like the label was going behind our backs and telling these guys what they wanted us to write. One guy was instructed by the label to "make sure Ariel's lyrics don't get too sassy." We weren't supposed to know that, but we saw it on an email he had pulled up on his computer for a second. Another one of the guys' brother was in a successful band with a female vocalist, and he began the session by playing me unreleased tracks off their upcoming album as a point of reference. I was taken aback that he saw "a girl singer" and took that to mean, "let's do a Paramore rip-off." We didn't end up writing anything together.

Another guy said he was instructed by the label to write a worship song with us for Christian radio. We were dumbfounded. I don't think he was supposed to tell us that. I argued with him for the entirety of the session about why that would never work for us and ended up feeling so sick that I had to stay home in bed the following day.

Songwriting was, and remains, freakishly personal for me. I wanted my songs to be so true that I could authentically sing them night after night on stage and feel good about them. I wanted to essentially dump my raw heart into a track and hope that other people *got it*. I wanted to make my audience feel the way my favorite bands made me feel.

I have a very clear memory of sitting on my bed listening to Linkin Park and making that connection: *These people understand me. Maybe one day I can make other people feel understood, too.* That specific moment has served me well over the years in instances when I might've second-guessed my passion. There have been times I've wondered why I'm doing this, if it's worth the effort, and I'm so grateful I have a clear, concrete memory to return to of why I wanted this in the first place. That memory drives me, fuels me, and reassures me that I'm pursuing something meaningful with my life.

At the same time, I didn't want to do everything that same way that my favorite bands did. They sang deep, dark, angsty songs that spoke to me, but that could be disadvantageous sometimes. Sometimes, when I was already really close to the edge, I didn't need their help pushing me over. Sometimes, when I was up to my eyeballs in despair, seeing my heroes expressing the same feelings that I had was comforting but not especially constructive.

I wanted to do the same emotional and compelling thing that they did so well—grabbing their listeners by the heart and saying *I see you*—but I didn't want to leave it at that. Once I had that audience, I had to take them somewhere. Somewhere a little further, lighter, better.

That's not easy to do. Most of the music I'd heard that had any sort of "positive" spin was cheesy religious pop music, which I had no interest in making. It's shaky ground, trying to gain a listener's ear and then trying to take them into a better state with you—and all within a three-minute track. You have to establish the trust first, and the best way I know how to do that is to get vulnerable. Show your fears, your weak spots, and people will almost always resonate with that. Once they're with you, once you've got them, then you have to be very careful not to lose them with some sort of "And then I found hope and now everything is better!" line thrown in at the end. No. You have to show the audience that you're not a salesman—that you're just a human. Not pushy, not desperate. Just an honest, "here's what sometimes worked for me" but in the most real and artistic way you can think of. If you do it right, the audience won't know that you sort of just bait-and-switched them, because the switch was presented so authentically and genuinely that they're happy to come with you. Many songs don't do this well, and it's the easiest part to screw up. People can smell bullshit from the back of the venue.

The co-writing thing wasn't my cup of tea, but I made it work by letting the co-writer focus on music and structure while I hoarded the lyrics to myself. The label was paying for our album, so I did my best to appease them. Unfortunately, this keep-the-label-happy dance we were trying to do kept getting more painful as we started to see how their agenda was drastically different from our own.

I find that a lot of people don't understand how labels really work. I know I didn't at the beginning. A record label is a glorified bank, and you are probably better off getting a loan from an actual bank. At least

Wells Fargo isn't gonna tell you how to run your business or what you can and cannot say in your songs. It became increasingly apparent that T&N didn't care one bit that we wanted nothing to do with the Christian market. They wanted us to make them lots of money. And we did. Our debut album, *Scripted*, broke the record for highest selling album by a debut artist on their label. We worked hard, toured our asses off, and figured it would pay off sometime.

It did pay off—for them. We did the math, and the volume of records we'd sold meant that they were making bank and we were supposed to start getting checks any day now. This is called "recouping." The labels front the money, and when your album sells enough to equal that amount, you're recouped and you start seeing checks in the mailbox.

Theoretically.

I don't want to badmouth anyone specific at T&N, because that's not mature or professional. (Read: they could sue me.) But let's just say it became increasingly apparent that we didn't see eye to eye on anything. The A&R guy who we'd had all the preliminary phone calls with about our vision quit the same day we started recording our album, and we had no one there to vouch for all those verbal promises he had made. Before we knew it, our CD was being sold at big money Christian bookstores across the country and our songs were being featured on Christian compilation CDs. I hear *Scripted* was a big hit at youth groups. We were safe enough for the adults to play us and edgy enough for the kids to like us. Rock on.

It shouldn't have surprised anyone when offers from various national Christian festivals came rolling in. Icthus Fest, Creation Fest, Cornerstone—they all wanted to book us for their event. For like two thousand bucks a show. Damn! Despite the money, I explicitly remember voicing my concern to the label (and my bandmates, and my mom, and anyone else who would listen) about accepting these offers. Wouldn't this seal our fate in the Christian music world forever? Wouldn't this be totally counterintuitive for us? Wasn't this just a bad idea overall? Nope, the label assured me. Nobody in the mainstream scene knows or cares what's happening in the Christian scene. Take the offer, make lots of fans, and sell that record that we paid for.

Um, okay.

It's not like we had any better offers waiting for us. If we didn't play these shows, we might not play many shows that whole summer. The label told us we needed to take these offers and show them we were serious so that they would then feel confident about promoting our album. I guess the hundreds of shows we'd already played on our own weren't convincing enough. Shawn and Adam were so unfamiliar with the Christian music scene (full disclosure: they didn't even know it existed, much less what it was), and they figured it was harmless. To be honest, the idea of such high-paying shows was kind of exciting for all of us. It felt like this thing we were doing was really working. We had hustled and grinded it out in ugly rock clubs for years, so if Creation Fest wanted to give us a couple grand to play for thirty minutes, we weren't really in a position to turn them down.

We played the shows. We brought our DIY work ethic to these shiny, clean festivals and were usually the only band taping up a hundred posters with our set times, talking to kids one on one about watching our show, and selling our own merch. I set up my sewing machine and began making custom tutus on the spot, gathering a crowd and a healthy little business on the side.

It worked. We played in front of some of the biggest crowds we had ever seen. Our signing line after the sets took hours to get through, and we made a lot of awesome fans and sold plenty of albums and t-shirts. The festivals seemed impressed and were eager to invite us back next year, on bigger stages and for even more money. We may have very well accepted those killer offers, save for a couple of things that made us pause.

I was crying myself to sleep every night. I was literally curled up on my bench in the van bawling my eyes out, my heart breaking at the thought of our promising, lucrative future. Nothing felt right. It felt off, gross, soul-sucking. Not exactly how I pictured feeling while living my dream.

I didn't truly believe in the Christian music industry. I had been exposed to plenty of it growing up, and getting to see behind the scenes as an artist made me suspicious of the whole industry. I couldn't understand how those songs were really helping and connecting with people if they were being created for and marketed to such a specific audience that was already primed to receive the message these songs were putting out over and over again. I wanted our music to impact people who were at their life's edge, not attending a shiny, clean Christian music festival. I couldn't bring myself to write songs that were unrealistically positive or wrapped up with a religious takeaway at the end, which struck me as contrived and inauthentic. I wanted to express my raw soul in my songs and connect with people who resonated with it, not write to a formula that guaranteed a specific subgroup of listeners—listeners I didn't really see myself in.

These feelings had been brewing in me for years, but I didn't know how to express them to my bandmates. I finally had a straight-up breakdown one night when we were piled into the van, driving through some God-forsaken hills in Utah somewhere. Shawn was driving, and everyone else was asleep except me, because I was doing my thing where I sobbed quietly on the bench and tried not to wake anyone while scolding myself for being so ungrateful for all these awesome opportunities. But the hurt won out.

I crawled up into the passenger seat next to Shawn and tried to make him understand.

"I can't do this anymore. It's killing me," I said.

We had had these conversations before, but this time he heard the conviction in my voice, saw the raw fear in my eyes. And he said okay.

"Okay what?"

"Okay, we won't play these kinds of shows anymore."

I was shocked. I'd been going on about this for at least a year, trying to get Shawn and Adam to understand how I felt about it. But Adam (who was an outspoken atheist) didn't get it, and Shawn (who served as our accountant) knew we couldn't survive without these shows.

Six months earlier, I had written about my feelings and posted it on my blog. The post was called "The Christians Are Driving Me Crazy." It made a lot of our fans mad, and I was sad for that, but I still agree with the thrust of that post—music shouldn't belong to one religious category. At least not my music. After I wrote that post, our fans started having conversations with me about it at shows. It was awkward. We'd be playing at a church and some kid would let me know he knew I didn't believe in playing churches.

One time, at Creation West, a fan point blank asked me about it. "I know you aren't into this sort of stuff, so why are you here, then?" It was a great question. If only I could have made him understand that we *had* to be here—that the label wouldn't market our album if we didn't play these shows and that we couldn't afford to keep making music if we didn't tour, and really, everyone kept telling me it *wasn't a big deal*.

But that kid was right. What were we doing there? What was I doing, making fans and connections that I didn't even feel good about? It was so slimy—using the Christian fanbase for their availability and pockets with the intention of moving on as soon as we could get the label to market us in the mainstream music category like we'd wanted all along. Cause that's what we were doing, wasn't it?

It all felt bigger than me, like it wasn't up to me somehow, and who was I to turn down these amazing, passionate fans? Who was I to ask Adam and Shawn to limit our band's success just because I felt so out of place in this scene?

But that night with Shawn in the front seat of the van, I didn't care anymore. Ethically, being in the Christian music space felt *wrong*. I couldn't do it anymore. I would have rather risked being selfish and asking the band to trust me than to keep suffering like I was.

I will always remember that night, because a lot of things changed moving forward. We committed to not playing any more religious shows, and we never did. We called our manager and broke the news, and he found us a powerful booking agent from New York who books the likes of Linkin Park and Hollywood Undead. Our fanbase starting evolving, and I started feeling at home in my band again.

I am so proud of myself for putting my foot down that night. For realizing that a lot of things were still out of my control, but that I could choose to stop participating in a life that was killing me. It was a powerful lesson: I can change things. My voice matters. I don't have to mindlessly do what everybody asks of me.

I also realized that I had to be a very vocal, active participant in my own life if I wanted to be happy living in it. I should have spoken up earlier, but I was scared of being perceived as a bitch or the bossy lead singer or whatever. I was scared of everything I'd lose, of all that everybody would lose. Still, I decided that would be the last time I'd let other people run my life. I decided I didn't really care if T&N was behind our record or not, because feeling good about the life I was living was infinitely better than selling records.

CHAPTER 6

WHEN SUCCESS ISN'T ENOUGH

I was on a plane, and I was flying to Amsterdam. This is where I was when this story began. This is the part where I stumbled onto the magic of loving myself.

This was such a defining event for me simply because, before that moment, I didn't know it could get any better. I thought beating self-harm as a teenager was about as good as it got. I thought not crying uncontrollably anymore constituted a Really Big Win. I had beaten the depths of despair, I had clawed myself out of my pity hole, and I was free.

Except that, you know, I wasn't. Turns out that "not wanting to die" and "happy" are not actually the same thing, which was a little disappointing to realize after all the work I'd done. When I was on the plane, I was kind of flatlining mentally and emotionally—I had done all I knew how to do, and it wasn't enough. You can't just stop passionately hating yourself; you have to fill that void with something. There's more. More freedom, more joy, more sanity.

And I wanted it. All of it. But how?

~~~

As the band continued to grow, it became annoyingly clear that *I had to make my own happiness.* I was finally living the life that I'd been dreaming about for years, but it wasn't exactly working like it was "supposed to." I was still messed up inside, and I couldn't rely on my music to save me.

Honestly, all my aspiring musicians out there should just skip this next part, because it's a major buzzkill.

Here's the deal: I am not rich or famous, but I am the lead singer of a successful rock band, so I'm pretty much technically a rockstar. This has given me unique insights into the topic of fulfillment, and also an up-close, firsthand answer to questions like, "Does being a rockstar make you happy?"

Nope.

I know, you're the exception. You were born to make music and your soul won't rest until you do. You were uniquely designed to do this and you belong up on that stage, sharing your artistic heart with your audience. You don't even need to be like, super-mega famous to be happy; you just need a core group of fans who've got your back and come to your shows and care about your music, and then you'll be happy for the rest of your life.

I know you, because I am you.

Not only has being a rockstar not made *me* happy, it also hasn't made my musician friends and touring mates happy either. Seriously. We've got our fragile egos and emotional instabilities, too. How do you think we write those songs we do? We may not be teenagers anymore, but that doesn't mean that we've somehow magically grown out of our demons just because we're older. A lot of us are mad at life because we made it to the top and it didn't actually fix anything.

Whenever we get a chance to tour with a really big band, I watch them closely. I spy on them from the side stage and eavesdrop on their conversations in catering. I try to see past the illusion to learn what's on the other side of the big, cool rockstar persona. I have had the privilege of growing close to some of these people and engaging in real conversations, and I sometimes get to see them for who they really are.

My first instinct when we were first starting out was to look at a successful band and envy them, assuming they've got it all made. Look at all those fans lining up to see you! Oh my gosh, you're selling thousands of dollars of merch every night! Your label is literally spending *millions of dollars* promoting you! You have a tour bus with a professional studio in it! I would, like, be sooooo happy if I were you!

But, of course, I would be wrong. You have all that stuff and you are clearly still unhappy. Like I said, I watch you, and this is what I see:

You stumble into the venue at two in the afternoon, wearing sweatpants and looking mega hung over from the night before. Load-in is taking forever and sound check is delayed, and so you're taking out your frustration on your crew. The stage is too small to use the full light rig, so you're up on stage cursing out your tour manager for approving this venue in the first place. The promoters are taking a huge merch split, ticket sales were just okay, and you're telling your bandmates about how the night is gonna suck. You make yourself sit through mandatory interviews where you're asked the same questions you've answered a million times before. You sneak out to the back alley, where I hear you fighting with your girlfriend on the phone for an hour. She's upset that you're on the road so much.

You head to the pre-show meet-and-greet and sit through another hour of fake smiling for the cameras and pretend to be interested in another story about how everyone is "your biggest fan." Then it's time to get on stage and force yourself to care about the audience that showed up that night, but all you're really noticing is the half-empty balcony. Headbang at all the right parts, smirk when the crowd cheers loudest for the washed-up single that you're sick and tired of, tear into the mic in agony for the emo song, then pray to God the crowd doesn't want an encore.

Your only private space is a six-foot hole with a curtain. You can't walk outside your bus unless you clean yourself up and are in the mood for dealing with the over-eager fans wanting more pictures. Your bandmates have no boundaries and are leaving their crap everywhere. Your label is pouring all of their money into promoting the newest cool band and you're probably going to get cut. You have no real social skills because the only conversations you have are with your crew and fans, and you feel completely isolated. You spend most of your time scrolling through Twitter, seeing how many likes your last Tweet got. You go to sleep, drunk and bored, and get to do it all again in a new city tomorrow.

No, this doesn't happen to every successful musician, and I know that these things probably sound like luxury problems. You'd kill to have an actual tour to complain about. You'd wake up every morning and just be grateful to get to play a show, right?

If you think that reaching your dream will suddenly make you happy when you haven't been before, think again. Success will just widen any cracks that were already there. If you were a little bit selfish before, success will make you a total asshole. If you were unsure of yourself before, success will turn you into a paranoid, insecure fraud. Your dream won't fix you. Only you can do that.

That's why success is the ultimate illusion. Reaching your goal will be pretty amazing, but it will not be the magic pill that solves all your problems. You can only enjoy living your dream if you're already healthy and strong.

I have met some genuinely happy people in this industry—guys who love the woman they've left back home and stay faithfully committed to her through all the crazy touring business. Musicians who go to their AA meetings on the road and don't drink the free liquor constantly being offered to them. Artists who are kind to their fans, who really love them, and who light up when they get to talk with them.

The musicians who can enjoy their success already all seem to have a deep, internal foundation of strength and self-love. Selling out an arena isn't their identity; it's just a cool bonus. Their external success is all just *frosting*. They've built their real life on solid stuff like family and genuine friends and their spirituality. They're humble, genuine, and kindhearted. They don't confuse their job with who they are or take themselves too seriously.

The good news is that success and joy are not at odds, and they can coexist—but they don't automatically arrive together. They have to be cultivated separately. This brings me to the bad news: if success doesn't create happiness, then that means we have to learn to make our own. If being loved and adored by fans can't fix our self-esteem issues, then we have to learn to fix them ourselves.

~~~

Rock & roll is the only job I know of where you get to write about all your issues and people will love you for it. You give language to people's agony, and those same people will follow you to the moon and back. Here's where this gets a little weird: If your entire career is riding on your despair, then how on earth are you supposed to ever be happy?

This used to make me nervous. I was worried that at some point I'd have to choose between being an authentic, honest, real musician and a happy one. That sucked. I wanted it all! I wanted the vulnerability and the impact *and* the sane, happy human part. I'd had enough of the miserable depression crap; my patience for that was maxed out.

Our band had gathered a tribe comprised of fans that related to our lyrics about life's darknesses, but I was desperately craving more light. Not being depressed is one thing, but actually being happy? It's risky stuff. You could become One of Those People. The white-washed, plastic people who smile too much and wear polo shirts and are annoyingly peppy all the time. No, thank you. I had no interest in losing touch with the deep, artistic parts of myself in the name of winning the happiness game.

There had to be a middle ground that I just hadn't found yet.

In the winter of 2012, we took our first little break from touring and began writing our second record. The writing process was different this time around in part because we had an actual fan base waiting for it. We also had a manager who was able to protect us from some of the BS that had happened during the creation of our first album. We were writing this one without the "help" of co-writers, and we were able to pick our own producer—within budget; of course.

That winter, I sat myself down in front of my beloved keyboard and I started to write. Just like the last time, I wanted every word to connect with our listeners. But this time, things were a little different. I was a little different.

All the work I'd been doing on myself since I'd had my realization that I wanted to be happy in my life was actually, well, working. I was reading inspiring books, learning to pay attention to my thoughts, and was feeling gradually better because of these things. But I couldn't exactly write about that, could I? I was torn. I didn't want to contrive anything in order to make a "deep" song happen, but I also didn't want to have to go around singing about rainbows and unicorns just because I was getting more stable internally.

So I just did what I've always done: cram my heart into a melody in the most unfiltered way I knew. It turns out that I still had a lot of shit inside me to sort through. Like, *a lot*. I was in absolutely zero danger of running out of writing material because my soul was just as dark and brooding as it always had been. I realized in that moment that I have to *fight* to be happy. I do not have to fight to be in pain. Pain is my default. Also, my work does not suffer from my joy. This realization was a big relief. I was able to write lyrics that were authentic, relatable, and maybe even a little bit helpful to somebody.

You can be happy. You can be happy and write about your pain at the same time, and that doesn't make you a liar. The truth is that the human experience is filled with pain just as it's filled with joy.

I can access my inner pain in a heartbeat; it's still there, it just doesn't own me anymore. Pain is a form of creative currency, and we have a limitless supply. We can access our pain on demand, without living in it round the clock. We can make interesting things out of our mess.

That's what artists do.

~~~

The more success our band experienced, the more the pieces started to come together. I was discovering firsthand that my suspicions were accurate—external momentum didn't impact internal misery on its own. I wanted to be growing my heart right along with my band.

It took that magical plane moment for me to realize that the way I felt about myself was overwhelmingly responsible for my lack of happiness. I had come a long way, sure, but the old mindsets still ran the show—the same poisons still lingered in my bloodstream. I had simply learned to manage it better, to be a "grown up" about it. It was duller, foggier—it was background unhappiness instead of intense despair. But it still droned on and on, sucking the life out of me without me even realizing it.

I'm generally not one to make sweeping generalizations on life based on my own personal experiences, but here's what I think:

We pretty much all hate ourselves in some way, and none of us know it because it's so normal that it's never observed, questioned, or discussed. We live our lives in a fog, and we don't know that the thoughts in our own heads are sucking the life out of us.

That is our normal. We usually don't say that we hate ourselves—we just know we're not happy. Self-hatred comes out sounding something like:

"I'm miserable."

"My life sucks."

"I'm bored."

"I feel numb."

"I wish I were different."

We think we hate our crappy, mundane lives, but that's really just a side effect from hating ourselves. I know this is true; when we start learning how to love ourselves, our "crappy" lives start getting a whole lot more enjoyable. Once you start loving yourself, stuff starts to take care of itself. No lie.

Do you believe me?

Maybe you feel like "self-hate" is a little too loaded of a word, and as far as you're aware, you don't actively, regularly hate yourself. You might not have a lot of compelling proof, like I did. You might not have scars up and down your limbs or torso from hurting yourself. You might not have journals full of self-loathing prose. You might not even sit and obsessively chat with your friends about what a loser you are. I don't know—maybe you're one of the lucky ones who didn't get this particular sickness, and you're fine and feel pretty good about yourself. In that case, you can close the book and go screw yourself (100% kidding; I think it's really great that you like yourself.)

But for the rest of us, the ones who live most of our lives with a steady background drip of misery and don't know what is wrong with us, well, finally feeling at peace with who we are is the magic elixir we've been looking for since we were born. It's everything.

Just to make sure we're on the same page here, "not intensely hating yourself" is definitely not the same thing as "actively loving yourself." When you actually like yourself, it's like all of life opens to you. It seems as though your whole world has a completely different feel to it, and everything feels brand new to you. Most of the issues in my life dissolve when I actively move from an attitude of self-disgust to one of self-celebration, and the ones that don't dissolve suddenly seem more manageable.

~~~

Here are just some of the ways that learning to love myself has changed my life for the better (stick with me if this is feeling a little overly feel-good—I promise we're going somewhere you'll want to come along for):

1. I take better care of myself. Things like letting myself read novels, put on makeup when I want to, and eat healthy, yummy food. For a long time, I didn't think I was worth the good stuff. Letting myself feel worthy to make money, be successful, collaborate with other people I respect. Allowing myself to buy nice things (trivial things like pretty sleepwear and cute picture frames and novelty phone apps). Letting myself not work all the time, and being all right with "good enough" instead of trying to be mind-blowing all the time.

2. No longer self-harming. I actually notice now when little manifestations of this habit subtly sneak back in, like digging my nails into skin or clenching teeth. I acknowledge it and ease up when I catch myself doing it, because I don't do that to myself—to someone I love—anymore. I have compassion for myself.

3. I let myself enjoy the different parts of my personality. I really love my brain and all its ideas. I love learning about myself, and I love figuring out how to work with rather than against myself. I love the fact that I care about other people and don't want anyone to feel worthless. I have some really awesome qualities, and I recognize these on purpose.

4. I am generally at peace with how I look and am mindful of what kinds of things threaten that. When I identify them, I eliminate them.

5. I'm not so hard on myself, and I no longer feel guilty all the time. There's grace when I mess up; I could work on this more, but I know I'm getting better all the time. Instead of constantly searching for or being worried about God, my connection to God is all around me. It makes me feel like I have the stamp of "I'm okay" from my creator; like somebody bigger than me decided I was a good idea. I feel safe and loved.

I want you to experience all that goodness, too, and if I could I'd give you step-by-step instructions in a heartbeat. The thing is, though, that loving yourself is an inside job. Nobody can love you for you. I can't even tell you how to do it. What I can do is tell you how *I* do this: how I break through my own self-loathing issues and replace the crazy with compassion.

THE WORLD WE LIVE IN IS DESIGNED TO HELP US HATE OURSELVES

Over and over, track on repeat, there's something wrong with me. Magazines, TV ads, social media—they all continually remind me that I'm broken in subtle and not-so-subtle ways. For a long time, almost every message I sent to myself echoed these sentiments: I am an unlovable, stupid mess. And that's exactly what society wants me to believe, because that's how people sell each other things. Advertisers count on me feeling this way about myself, because otherwise I wouldn't need to buy what they want to sell me. Me believing that I am inherently jacked up makes the capitalist world go 'round. And I am a very powerful player in this system.

It starts with buying into this "I am broken, and I need fixing" message, and then somehow turns into me buying the new shade-match-technology-with-anti-aging-shimmer foundation that they want to sell me. My low self-esteem is creating jobs, putting food on the CEO's table (or yachts in their private ocean or whatever), and generally driving the beast.

The world runs on self-hatred.

They *got me*, guys. They hook me, day after day after day. They've probably hooked you, too. But I wouldn't feel too bad, because they spend billions of dollars and thousands of research hours annually trying to trick us and get inside our heads and figure out how to help us hate ourselves. You'd have to be superhuman to come out unscathed.

What I'm saying is this: we're screwed. The deck is stacked; we're gonna live our whole lives inundated with subliminal, soul-killing messages about what's wrong with us, and we're in no way equipped to resist.

But that's okay. I know a trick.

Since the whole freaking world is trying to fuck with me, I've drawn some lines in the sand. I've outlined the borders of where they can and cannot go. They can mess with my head, yeah, but they can't truly get inside of my actual heart. There's a spot inside of all of us that is safe—that is pretty much untouchable by the media and The Man and all that. All I have to do is remember that it exists, that *I* exist, and remember that *I am*.

The moment that I remember to feel my own energy, my *aliveness*—that is the moment I stop the crazy cycle and connect with something bigger. Something divine, something electric, something that feels like the whole freaking point of being alive. Something that has nothing to do with anti-aging shimmer foundation.

In his bestselling book *The Power of Now*, Eckhart Tolle calls this feeling *the joy of being*.[2]

Isn't that great? The joy of being. It's this idea that the awareness of being alive is enough to be cause for joy. The world can't touch that. It can't take one step near that without your permission.

I've spent so much of my life hating the fact that I exist, mad at myself for my own wretched *aliveness*, and here's this concept that suggests that I find joy in the simple fact that I exist! It's madness. My initial response to this was, "Well, I'm alive, but I don't feel a whole lot of joy about that fact, so I must be doing it wrong."

And I would venture to say to my past self that *yes, darling, you were doing it wrong*.

Because being alive is cause for celebration. Being a player in this universe is a privilege. We get a part in the show. We get a shot at this! We count. And that's exactly why, paradoxically...

---

[2]Eckhart Tolle. *The Power of Now: A Guide to Spiritual Enlightenment.* Vancouver, BC: Namaste Publishing, 2004.

THE WORLD WE LIVE IN IS ALSO TRYING TO TEACH US HOW TO LOVE OURSELVES

The world is waiting for us to realize how wonderful and valuable we are. The sun is located at precisely the correct distance to warm our bodies and grow our food without burning us to death. We are at the top of the food chain, the center of the ecosystem. I look at the beauty of changing leaves in the fall, I taste a ripe mango in the summer, and for a brief second, I wonder if the universe is trying to tell me something. *You matter!* I hear it whisper. *This is all for you. Don't hold back. Burn bright, baby!*

Both messages—the world wants you to hate yourself and the world wants you to love yourself—are getting through, and they both play in my subconscious night and day. I can turn one up louder than the other, and I can choose to believe one over the other. I want to believe that all of creation is rooting for me. I want to feel welcome on this planet, to feel loved and cherished. I let myself choose gratitude, overwhelmed by this amazing place I get to call my home—even when things are so difficult I feel like giving up.

Life loves you. The world is bursting at the seams with love and guidance for you. Pick that one.

~~~

It does something strange to me when I am reminded that, for so many of us, self-hatred is our around-the-clock reality. I sat in on a casual meditation meetup on a tour last summer as Buddy, vocalist for Senses Fail, led us in a few precious minutes of guided meditation. It was cute to watch my sweaty, tired, tatted friends and coworkers (that had been screaming bloody murder into a mic in front of thousands a few hours earlier) sit outside in a circle and listen to their breathing while dozens of local crew members tore down stages and cursed into their hand-held radios all around us. It was an honest attempt at finding stillness amidst the chaos.

Buddy had us all sit in the silence—or as silent as it could be with drills and trucks and workers buzzing all around us—and occasionally threw out a few guiding phrases to help keep us present. At the end of the meditation session, he asked how the experience had been for us. One of the guys spoke up about how it was difficult to sit with himself that long. Another guy mentioned that he was met with a really strong sense of his anxiety, and it occurred to him just how often he lived from that anxious place.

I knew what Anxiety Guy meant—I could relate to that feeling of, "Wow, I'm even harder on myself than I thought I was. I don't like spending this time with myself." It kinda broke my heart as we went around the circle and more people shared stories of how difficult it was to be gentle with themselves in their own heads and to not use this moment of stillness as a prime opportunity to beat themselves up.

Hating ourselves is the great personal epidemic of our time, and this straight up freaks me out. It messes with my head when I see someone who looks totally fine admitting that they are full of self-hatred. *Really? You too?! Well shit.*

It's the same all across the board, and not even the people you think might have it all are immune. Rockstars hate themselves. CEOs hate themselves. Kindergarten teachers hate themselves. This is our global inner life, and I want to be a part of changing it starting with my own little self-love revolution.

When I was 17, I started putting the pieces together and realized that all my friends and I were depressed. We had all had painful lives in varying ways, and we all felt somehow unqualified for happiness or success. *Everyone* was *exceptionally* messed up, which of course makes no sense. *Miserable is the new normal.* When I began to see this reality clearly, things clicked for me. It made me feel like my story wasn't worse than anyone else's, so maybe I could have a shot at joy. It took away all my excuses, invalidating my reasons for being the victim. It would take a few years before these mindset shifts worked their way into my life in more practical ways, but I was beginning to see the light.

It's the same with this self-love thing. When I realized, "Oh, we're all in our own heads all day beating ourselves up? We're all just going around hating ourselves?" I was like, well, screw that. I wanna skip that part and just go after joy, thanks very much.

This all may sound like an oversimplification, but this really is how a lot of the powerful change in my life has happened. Just a sudden, subtle thought shift can change the course of your whole life.

As I started figuring out that loving myself could pretty much fix everything, I began getting more and more interested in the specifics. "Just love yourself" sounds nice and all, but what does it actually look like? Does it mean I'm happy all the time? Does it mean I blindly embrace everything about myself, including my flaws that I'd rather work on and change for the better? Is there a chance I could go too far with it and get all stuck up about it? All these questions kept bouncing around in my head, and even though I've been working on this self-love stuff for a while now, I still definitely don't have all the answers. I do know this: Loving ourselves isn't nearly as tough as we think it is.

Sometimes I feel like if I'm not SUPER EXCITED to be MY WONDERFUL SELF ALL THE TIME, then I'm not loving myself properly. But I don't think that you have to walk around feeling the epic surge of love for yourself all day, because that's not how love works with anyone else. After you've known someone for a while, the crazy butterflies calm down and your love for them is evident mostly with your actions and how you treat them. Yeah, you'll still feel that fluttery surge for them sometimes, too, but that's probably not gonna be your default mode.

You don't have to strive to always feel head-over-heels in love with yourself in order to practice self-love. You can show yourself love by your actions.

What I really love about this truth is that I don't have to depend on something as shifty and unstable as my feelings to determine whether or not I'm currently loving myself. I can easily choose to do small, concrete actions that set up my life as a place that makes me feel welcome and, yes, loved. I'll tell you all about some of my favorite go-to's for this later on, but before we get there, let's get some of the resistance stuff out of the way.

I really hate to say this, but you should probably expect some major resistance from within on this road to loving yourself. Expect your inner critic to be fighting you every step of the way. That same way you cringe inside when you hug someone that you don't actually like? It's like that, and it's gonna feel very counterintuitive and kind of cheesy to shower yourself in praise and compassion when you've spent your whole life knee-deep in the self-hatred swamp. So just get comfortable with the weirdness—don't fight it.

I feel especially qualified to address different kinds of resistance to loving myself, because I'm a bit of a pro. I've mastered the art of taking something wonderful and ripping it to shreds while coming up with all the reasons why it won't work for me. I've hand-picked a few of my favorite, stickiest lies and spelled them out for you here in the hopes that you might identify some similar thought patterns in yourself. Then we can kick those lies to the curb together.

Worthiness

I know. I get it. I can practically hear you thinking it. Gosh, I can hear *myself* thinking it. It sounds like this:

"I am not worthy of love. I am my own special brand of fucked up and I don't qualify. Trying to love myself would make me feel even stupider than I already do. I was born screwed up. After entering the world, I screwed up even more. I am one big screw up. I don't get to make the cut. I don't get to love myself."

Just get it all out, sweetheart. In fact, I would love for you to join me and write out your very own reasons why you do not deserve love, and why directing any love towards yourself is a complete waste of time. I would really take advantage of this chance if I were you—do it now, before your self-hate can elbow in and yell, "this is bullshit!" at you. For inspiration, because I'm inspiring like that, here are some of my favorite reasons why I "can't" love myself:

I should be farther along in life.

I still care what people think of me.

I am ungrateful for my awesome life.

My face looks blotchy without makeup and my hair is damaged.

My tone of voice is childish.

I ask too much of my bandmates.

I judge other people.

I fall into depression even though my life is good.

I get excited about projects but can't see them through.

I let my feelings run my day.

I think about myself too much.

I get sad too easily.

I don't keep the house clean enough.

I'm too hard on myself.

"I'm too hard on myself" is especially awesome. Nothing better than beating yourself up for beating yourself up, am I right?

Okay, friend, your turn. This'll be easy. Make a list of all the reasons why you can't love yourself (if you want to write right in the book, go ahead! That is, if you've already bought a copy. If you just picked this bad boy up off the shelf at Barnes & Noble, maybe take a trip to the cashier first. Cheers.):

Great job—seriously! Now put this book down and rest your beautiful, brave heart. Make a mug of your favorite tea or coffee (the kind you've been saving for company), take a nice little walk, or paint your nails. Basically, do something light and relaxing. You deserve it. From there, you could do any number of things. For example, you could burn your list (crazy cathartic, but maybe a touch extreme), or you could rip it out of the book and tape it to your bathroom mirror so you never, *ever* forget just how unlovable you are (the other extreme on the spectrum of options).

I'm gonna suggest you do neither. I want you to leave that list right where it is, in the safety of this book. It'll be like a time capsule for your self-hating ways, becoming more and more outdated and confusing and bizarre with each year. Flip back to it if you want to, or never look at it again—it's your choice.

But first, a few more classic resistance responses.

Self-Love is a Narcissistic Waste of Time

I'm scared that this whole self-love thing is really selfish, and nobody's had the guts to tell me yet. My inner critic says "Yeah, no shit it's selfish, look at you obsessing over yourself and the way you feel about yourself. Nobody cares! You don't have time for this; grow up and go do something useful with yourself." My heart is tempted to cower down and reply, *Omg, you're right, I'm so sorry, my bad, I always mess this stuff up, I'll shut up now.* Then I feel so silly, so stupid, for thinking that maybe for a second there I was worth taking good care of.

Not only do I hear these negative things inside my head all the time, but I'm also afraid that somebody will actually walk up to me and say these things to my face one day. To make things really twisted, I like to beat this imaginary person to the punch, so I make sure I keep my list of my messed-up-ness always on hand for easy reference. I figure that, if this imaginary person ever does call me on it, I'll be so ready. I will beat them to it. "Yes, I know that I'm the most self-centered person in the world! I'm totally wasting my time thinking about myself, right? Here, let me help you out, I have a whole bunch of really great reasons why I'm so not worthy of self-love, let me show you!"

If you can relate to this, I feel for you. It's a crappy place to be, because loving yourself is the most important thing you can do in your whole entire lifetime. Some of you will have a really hard time with this. That's okay. Just let yourself consider this possibility: Your purpose on Earth is to love…yourself.

"But what about everyone else?! What about the starving babies and the giant pandas and the sea turtles who choke on our garbage in the ocean?!"

They deserve love, too. Love isn't a finite resource. It's cool.

This is classic guilt-addict thinking. Guilt addicts harness their guilt and use it for fuel to get everything done in life. They think that their guilt serves them, and that without it they'd never do anything great until one day, they wake up and realize that this is a stupid, soul-sucking way to live, and that it actually doesn't help the starving babies or pandas at all because they're too busy feeling so freaking guilty about everything all the time. You can't be all that helpful to the people and issues in your life and world that need you when you live like that.

I finally realized that I had to be healthy in order to offer anybody anything, and I see now that me loving myself is doing the world a great service, because I am adding to the love in the world.

So start with you. Start by making you a healthier, happier place to live, and then spread the love. Along the way, you will inspire tons of others on accident when they see your brilliance and strength shining through, no longer inhibited by some dark cloud of self-hatred and guilt. Loving yourself is the best thing that you can do with your time on this planet. Everything else flows out of that place.

Settling

This one goes something like this: "I can't love myself because then I'll have to settle for my awful, pathetic self! If I accept myself, I will stop trying so hard to be awesome and just become complacent and go nowhere in life."

Mmm-hmm. I know this one intimately, too. It is so scary to even imagine accepting myself, because what if I go too far and actually start liking the bad parts of myself, too? What if I decide it's okay to be rude when I feel like it? What if I decide I love my bare face in the morning and become one of those women who never wear makeup? What if I embrace my lazy side and then end up sitting on the couch scrolling Pinterest forever?

This is, in many ways, the perfectionist in you talking, and here's why this is crazy thinking: People like us, who naturally worry about settling, never have to *actually* worry about settling. Trust me. It is built into our DNA to want to do great things, to want to *be* great, and our true selves will most definitely step in and have a chat with us if we somehow take this self-love thing a little too far and go off the deep end. Trust your intuition, and trust the universe, here. Loving yourself is pure and good—even holy. It won't turn you into an obnoxious narcissist.

Also, here's the thing: True self-love inspires evolution.

Loving yourself doesn't mean that you fully accept yourself in your current state, set up camp, and stay there. On the contrary; constantly evolving is one of my favorite ways to *show myself* love. I let myself be inspired by other people, by art, by the amazing world we live in. I am always on the lookout for more ways to add joy to my life, whether that's through learning a new skill or actively improving my character flaws that I'm not content to live with. But I do these things lovingly, and I don't make myself feel bad for not having figured something out earlier.

Don't let fear of settling hold you back from totally loving yourself. When you love yourself, you keep changing and getting better almost as a side effect. Being open to change does not mean you are weak, or insecure, or a never-ending self-help project. Awesome people change. They become even more awesome. They change their minds and go back to what they originally wanted. Give yourself space to evolve— even to devolve—and revolve.

So, those are some of my faves. You might be really good at this, too, and have some solid reasons as to why self-love isn't for you. Enlighten me.

Self-love won't work for me because:

_____

_____

_____

_____

_____

_____

_____

In addressing our resistance to self-love, we are essentially calling out our own excuses. If you have tried to change in the past with little success to show for it, it may be time to get a little more serious with yourself. Sometimes a little tough love is required on the path to self-love.

When someone has been living in their pain cocoon, delicately nursing their wounds and creating sacred space for their sadness, a bit of tough love is the best way I know of to facilitate a wake-up call. They are in a sleepy, dreamy, extremely pained state of being, and in order to survive like that, they have to numb out on a regular basis. Sometimes you've just got to throw a bucket of ice-cold water all over their sorry story to snap them out of it long enough for them to see what's really going on. Long enough for them to see their reality with fresh, awake eyes.

This is often what I try to do with our music. Admittedly, I have to be mindful about not getting too intense or wordy in a three-minute track, but if I could say anything, here's what that would be:

Wake up! You do not have to live like this. If fact, you are *choosing* to suffer by saying yes to all this misery. Even though this is a hard pill to swallow, you *are* choosing to stay miserable by not doing anything about it. You will never, ever heal your aching heart by making a cozy home out of it for your sadness. I know life can suck, and I'm so, so sorry about that. I know you have probably had really unfair hands dealt to you. But it's time to bust out of the comforting cocoon you've woven around yourself and get to work making yourself a better place to live, because no one's going to do it for you.

You still with me?

This is the kind of bullish attitude we need when we first take on our own self-loathing. We need to come at it with a holy anger, a complete and total lack of tolerance for the parts of ourselves that are holding us back. This is how we interrupt the cycle of sadness long enough to let some light in and face our reality. Now, this doesn't mean you should hate yourself *more* for harboring these habits; it just means that it's time to recognize them for what they are and then to set them aside as things that no longer serve you.

This might not feel super warm and fuzzy—hell, it might not even feel like a loving way to treat ourselves. Before we get to all the good self-love stuff, though, we have to hate our current reality bad enough to change it. We have to be sick of our sickness and want to feel better way more than we want to stay where we are.

You probably have very good, convincing reasons to stay stuck, wherever "stuck" is for you. You probably have killer excuses why you're not qualified to live your dream or even be happy. Here's the kicker, though: We've all experienced immense pain. Yes, some people's situations are way more extreme than others', and some people have way more obstacles to overcome on their journeys out of their pain. What this doesn't mean is that your pain is somehow less or more worthy than anyone else's, or that you are somehow more or less deserving of recovery.

When I realized this, the inflamed wound inside me seemed to finally calm down and begin to heal when I saw how level the playing field really was. When I realized we were all out there screaming bloody murder for many of the same reasons, I put the knife down and stopped hacking away at my own life.

It was a hard pill to swallow, but I started to see that my friends and I could all be dealt the same hand (sketchy brain chemistry, less-than-stellar home lives, etc.), and we could do with that whatever we pleased. It didn't have to take any of us out. It didn't have to define us for the rest of our lives.

I finally had to make a conscious choice to move forward and stop acting like I was being held hostage by my own life. Not all my friends were into that decision. Some of them wanted to keep analyzing their problems with no plan for finding solutions and let their past keep leaking into the future. That was totally their choice, but not something that made sense to me anymore. I stopped having long, drawn-out conversations with them about my problems, and I didn't endlessly empathize with them when they kept rehashing theirs. My resolve to be happy seemed to make some of them nervous, and after a few years, we weren't as tight as we had been. I wish these friends and I could have stayed close, but I also don't regret deciding to take charge of my own life like I did.

It was worth it. Because I really wanted to feel better. And I still do. You have to want to feel better. You have to want to be healthy more than you want to be sick. You have to want to love yourself more than you want to hate yourself. That's what finding happiness is about.

So, here's my question for you: Do you want to get well?

PART 2
ART

CHAPTER 7

THE PRACTICALS OF SELF-LOVE STRATEGY

I hope that last chapter felt like taking a long, hot bath in all your toxic mindsets and beliefs about yourself. I hope you enjoyed purging and detoxing all that garbage, because now it's time to move on. It's time to get down to the really essential stuff: the reason we've come this far.

When you're in the process of becoming an *ex self-hater*, you need to accept the fact that your brain is a little warped, and that you've been living in a twisted reality. You've been, essentially, very sick. Now it's time to start living in the real world, or better yet, to begin crafting a world for yourself that you love living in. How do you do that?

I'm going to share exactly what's worked for me, and I want to make it very simple, because at the beginning of this journey, you need this stuff *spelled out for you*. You need it to be idiot-proof—not because you're an idiot, but because you've been believing lies for so long. All the demons in your head will conveniently serve up a million compelling reasons why taking good care of yourself is a total waste of resources, so you've got to be ready to offer some simple, effective counters when they do.

While I'm going for *simple* here, I can't say it will be easy. It's important that you know that up front. If you want real change in your life, you will have to do some of the hard stuff. Some stuff that lazy people don't want to do. Stuff resentful people simply can't do—yet. Stuff that most people don't know how to do. If loving ourselves were so easy, wouldn't we all have been doing it already?

Along the way, you will have to navigate some of the uncomfortable soul revelations that most people don't want to mess with. Go there. Be one of the ones who faces the hard stuff and breaks through to the other side. If you do, you will be unstoppable.

When you begin swapping out your old definitions of truth for new, better ones, you'll be able to watch your life changing before your eyes. Before we go down that road, let's set ourselves up for success. Let's get some quick wins under our belts so we can get a good sense of momentum going.

It's difficult to teach someone new beliefs, and it's even trickier to actually make yourself believe something that you don't...actually... believe. So, we're not gonna mess with that right away. Instead of spitting out a bunch of cute little affirmations and asking you to repeat them out loud until they stick (oh, we'll get to that), I want us to just skip that step for now and begin the process of changing our actual lives. It's much more fun that way, because who doesn't love instant gratification?

We are going about it backwards, on purpose. Most people suggest changing yourself from the inside out—first change your beliefs, and then watch your life change. Usually, I'm all about that. However, I've had a lot of success by going outside-in instead, rearranging my outside world so it constantly reminds me of how I want my inside world to feel. This is the perfect way to get buzzing about your new life as you begin to change your old mindsets, because you can take practical, measurable steps to add more love into your life. Trust me, *the way you treat yourself completely affects the way you feel about yourself.* By starting with simple, actionable ways to show yourself that you matter, you interrupt the self-loathing that has been your normal, and your heart will feel the difference.

~~~

As creative people, we tend to use our ideas to serve others; we come up with unique solutions to big problems, we create beautiful things, we use our gifts to better the world in some way. But we shouldn't forget that we have access to a goldmine of creativity that we can also use to help ourselves. In learning to love myself, I've been able to successfully channel my creativity into finding unique ways to make my life easier.

I've learned a few tricks as I've reprogrammed myself out of the self-hate spiral, because sometimes I really do have to *trick* myself into self-love when my circumstances or mental state go a little haywire. While I can't always envision the ideal life that I'm after, I *can* fill my world with maps and hints to help keep me on track. It helps to make it foolproof. Break it down, take out the mystery. Loving ourselves can be vague and unpractical, or it can be deliciously simple and fulfilling.

I've learned to let my external environment help me on this journey. I've set up a million little reminders of my value all over my physical world and filled the spaces around me with beacons of self-love.

Where do you start?

First, be on the lookout for things in your life that suck your energy, especially things that you can change. Once I started doing this, I found there were a lot of little, seemingly insignificant things that drained me to think about but that it never occurred to me to actually address. They seemed too small, too stupid, a waste of my time. But ignoring these things just reaffirmed the broken belief that my feelings towards something didn't matter unless my logic also deemed it "worthy of my time."

For example, I can't even tell you how many times a day I have found myself feeling bad about my nails. *My nails.* Don't judge. Actually, sure, go ahead and judge a teeny bit—it's a little weird. They have never been great; they chip and peel and anytime we're on the road they boast a layer of filth no matter how many times I clean them. Finally, I noticed how many times a day my nails came up in my thoughts, and I was like, "Oh, wow, I really care about this, don't I?" It surprised and somewhat embarrassed me that my nails were that big of a deal to me.

It took me a while to pay attention to this little thing that kept tapping on my shoulder day after day—I didn't get my first manicure until last year, and even then it was because someone bought me a gift certificate. When I finally got one, I was blown away by how happy it made me. It was as if a major problem in my life finally felt solved for a few precious days, or at least until the polish began to chip. Once I realized what a difference this made in my happiness levels, I felt much less resistance towards devoting some effort to this area of my life.

I get it now: Apparently, the state of my nails matters to me, and I don't have to fight it, even if my head doesn't really understand why I care and still kinda thinks nail salons are a lame way to spend time and money. Doesn't matter: my head doesn't get a vote on this. I am committed to treating myself with as much self-care as I can, and this is one of those things I guess I really like. So to the salon I will go, and I will let myself love it.

Just as you can take stock of what drains you in your life, you also want to be on the hunt for what lights you up. This is really fun. Look for little things that put a smile on your face, and make note of them as you find them. I call it Joy Hunting.

I want you to start keeping a list of really easy, accessible ways to spoil yourself throughout the day. Keep track of what brings a moment of bliss to your day, no matter how silly or trivial it may seem. That way, you always know what to do to cheer yourself up or give yourself a healthy reward for kicking ass on a project. For me, hot tea is one of my favorite things, and I absolutely love scented lotions. And *candles*, oh my gosh, candles are the best things in the world. You better believe I have a cabinet full of teas, a bathroom full of lotions, and a whole home filled with lit candles. I've made peace with these little things being a part of my life. I budget for them, and I don't let myself feel guilty for "wasting" the candles as I burn them or make a big deal about the time it takes to boil water for tea. I've decided I'm worth the effort.

Give yourself those moments, those indulgences. They help turn an ordinary life into a fabulous one, a dull day into a series of sacred moments. It's the little things in life, so go find your "little things" and stock up, use them, enjoy them!

In the interest of transparency, if I had read the above paragraph a few years back, I would have probably thought, "Seriously? I hate my life and you're telling me to boil water for tea? I've got better things to do." If that same thought crossed your mind, that's totally okay. Acknowledge your cynicism and call it out for what it is: the resistance that we talked about in Chapter 6. Our resistance is actually helpful in showing us the areas where we need the most love.

I notice this same resistance in myself all the time. Whenever I hear about and observe other people taking great care of themselves, it usually blows my mind—and the first thing I tend to do is judge them. I think, *That's not fair! You can't spend that much time/money/energy on yourself! Quit screwing with the curve, buddy. You're making the rest of us look bad.* Then I remember that, like me, they can do whatever the hell they want, and if I'm mad at them for "cheating" and taking really great care of themselves, then I'm just jealous because I want that for myself, too.

I want to suggest some easy ways you can set up your life and environment to serve you on your self-love journey. These things range from simple, ten-second additions to your day to more in-depth alterations you can make to serve your joy. Read through the following self-care ideas with an open mind, and pay attention to any that cause a strong reaction in you. Chances are, the ideas that make you think *well, that's totally ridiculous* are the same ideas that your subconscious self is craving.

LEVEL 1: EASY

Fun Water

Water is a big deal, and we should all probably be drinking lots more of it than we are. Whenever I feel a little itchy or keep returning to the kitchen looking for something but not sure what I'm looking for, I find that drinking water can help a lot. It's also a great thing to drink if you're feeling sleepy in the middle of the day. But normal water can get boring, so we want to jazz it up and make it special, because we're special like that. Try adding basil (really!) or mint leaves, lemon or lime slices, or cucumber or melon slices to fresh, pure water. Make up a new flavor combination. It'll change your life.

Post–it Notes

My Post-it notes serve as my trail of breadcrumbs that faithfully lead me back to sanity. At various times, you'll find them on my mirror, in my closet, hidden away in books, or tucked in a drawer, and they always have something lovely to say that points me back in the right direction. Try to keep a pad of Post-its nearby for moments of brilliance, for quotes that inspire you, or for little encouragements, and put those suckers up everywhere. Be sure to change them out regularly, too, because after you've seen or read a phrase too many times it tends to lose its personal meaning and resonance.

Pajamas

That's right, your sleepwear matters. While I won't tell you *not* to keep wearing your oversized Minnie Mouse sweatshirt from middle school with stains on it to bed, I am gonna make a case for why your PJ's matter a lot more than you think.

It's all about feeling good. If a hoodie does that for you, then go for it. But this is about way more than physical comfort (I'm sure that thing is as soft as a kitten by now); it's about what you wear for hours of your life, every single day! Don't minimize that. Your sleepwear is what you begin and end your day in, and how you start your day is really important.

When I finally understood this, I threw out all my extra-large band tees and began wearing things that made me feel cute to bed. I went out and bought actual sleepwear for the first time—for me, that was pretty, silky pajamas I felt awesome in. Before, I'd felt like a slob and unkempt in my big tees. Once I started wearing things I'd intentionally picked out for myself instead of stuff I'd just settled for, it changed how I looked at myself in the mirror in the mornings. I don't know, maybe this doesn't matter to you, but I was surprised to find that it does matter to me, and what a change I saw in myself. Your roommates or the man or woman in your life will probably notice, but even if they don't, give it a try and feel the difference it makes. It's just one more way to throw yourself some good self-care and remind yourself how valuable you are even as you climb into bed. It's been a long, wonderful day, and you deserve satin—or an oversized Slayer tee. Just maybe a new one.

Passwords

This next trick is one of those things that's very tiny and seemingly unimportant, but it can add up in a good way. You probably enter passwords online a dozen times a day, so make the experience something that helps center you and remind you of what matters rather than the name of your dog spelled backwards. Every time I unlock my computer, I can enter in a positive statement about my life, like "iamfabulous" or "ichoosejoy." This stuff helps, I promise. I love taking something as mundane and neutral as entering a password and turning that moment into a subtle reminder of where I'm going in life.

Self-Love Heroes

Pick some self-love heroes that inspire you. These are people, real or imagined, whom you are convinced have every reason in the world to love themselves because they're just undeniably awesome. Imagine what it feels like to be them, what they must think of themselves. You can mentally refer to them any time you need them, and ask yourself what they have that you don't—and I'm not talking about fancy cars or huge mansions or private security or anything like that. What about *them* do they seem to have that you don't? If they deserve to feel awesome about themselves, you do, too. Aspire to be a self-love hero for someone else one day.

An Extra Five Minutes

To get dressed, I mean. I have a closet full of clothes that I bought or made, technically like, and in theory should be able to throw pretty much any combination of which on and walk out the door feeling good. But I've learned that I can bring a whole new level of joy to my day by experimenting and finding a new, awesome outfit combination.

I like taking an extra five minutes on top of the sixty seconds it takes to throw on a pair of jeans and a top to try on different shoes to see which ones look and feel the best that day. I'll try on a scarf and see if that's working. I'll take a second and see which jacket is gonna tie the whole thing together. In the midst of this game of dress up, I'll realize that this outfit would look so much better with a different pair of jeans completely, and I'll change those before heading out the door. This way, I go through my day feeling like I really did my best with the wardrobe I've got, and I usually discover whole new outfit combinations that I never would've thought of if I hadn't given myself a few extra minutes to play around.

Smiling at the Mirror

Whenever I catch my reflection in a mirror, I like to smile at myself. My go-to reaction in the past has been to pick myself apart—a split end here, some smeared eyeliner there—but that was such an unloving way to interact with myself. Whenever I have the chance now, even if it's just when I'm washing my hands, I look up, look deep into my eyes, and smile. I approve of the woman standing in front of me, and I make sure she knows it.

LEVEL 2: MODERATE

Smoothies (and other power foods)

Smoothies make me alarmingly happy. I love waking up and throwing a few handfuls of frozen fruits, fresh spinach (don't knock it till you try it), and some juice into my badass Ninja blender and drinking up all that goodness as I go through my morning. If I can round up all-organic ingredients, even better.

Smoothies taste yummy, of course, but I take it to a whole new level of joy by really hyping them up for myself. I recognize that I am starting my day with powerful antioxidants and immune-boosting vitamins that will help keep me strong and focused all day. Taking a second to be aware of that as I enjoy my smoothie brings me even more pleasure than the flavors themselves. I like starting my day feeling unstoppable, and smoothies do that for me.

I encourage you to find some good-for-you breakfast foods that make you feel like you're killing it, whether that's a mushroom and red pepper omelet, a bowl of oatmeal with blueberries, a piece of toast with peanut butter and banana slices—whatever makes you feel healthy and kick-ass. Play around and discover what works for you.

Working Out

Working out is an especially powerful way to show yourself love. At times, I know it can feel more like forcing tough love on yourself than gentle compassion, but even when pushing our endurance limits, we don't beat ourselves into submission for the ultimate goal of a perfect body. We train our minds along with our bodies, and practice the discipline of gently introducing change into our lives. Your body deserves to be the object of loving care, to feel beautiful and strong. The more you make peace with yourself, the more you may find yourself wanting to get and keep your body moving, since endorphins help keep you feeling happy and calm.

A Beautiful Space

Your environment matters *so much*. Your surroundings impact your very soul, so make them beautiful. Having a clean and beautiful home is an amazing way to show ourselves love. It's like saying to yourself, "Hey, friend, you deserve to live in a habitable, beautiful space, so I'm committed to making that happen for you, even if it takes some effort."

Since I can't control that much of my environment while on tour, I've learned to set my home up to feel as inspiring and cozy as possible. I have pretty pictures on the walls, a tea display in my kitchen, and all my favorite, most beloved books lined up on my bookshelf. You don't have to spend a lot of money or go crazy on clutter, but don't devalue the effect that your living space has on you. You live there, after all— make it work for you.

Breaks

Tea or coffee or cocoa breaks. Snack time. Walks around the block. Naps. Days off. You might think this one belongs in the "easy" category, but let me assure you from personal experience that it does not. If you are like me and have a drill sergeant for a brain, then you will find it really challenging to give yourself the rest that your soul is craving.

I struggle with a twisted, false belief that I am somehow "above" breaks and that I can go forever. That my energy and ideas and hustle should never run dry, so I can always go longer/farther/harder than anyone else. Even if I've been running on empty for miles, I can always squeeze a couple more drops out, right? This belief has served me on numerous occasions when I've needed it (circa Warped Tour 2014), but it's also been a threat to my sanity. I'm not superhuman, and I'm not a special case that can just keep pushing onward indefinitely. I need to show myself love by treating myself like a *person* and saying to myself, *Hey, baby, you've been killing it at life. I'd love for us to take today off, no guilt. What do you say?*

You can—and should—do the same for yourself when you know you're running on empty.

A New Skill or Hobby

You know, just for fun. Not because you need to amp up your resume or in the name of self-improvement. You can be interested in something that has nothing to do with your career or lifestyle, and you can take the time to learn it. Whether learning a new instrument that you'll probably never play in your band or cooking a new dish just because you want to, it's really nice to show yourself love by learning something new. You're telling yourself, "I care about what you're curious about. I'm willing to invest time into letting you explore this to see if we like it."

Another upside of just-for-fun activities is that they can be used as a funnel of sorts for negative or unwanted energy. Try channeling your creative superpowers to redirect pent-up emotions into something lighthearted and whimsical, and see how your feelings can change.

Makeup

This is only for those of you who enjoy wearing makeup, if that's something that feels good to you. But if you see some great eye shadow art on Pinterest and want to try it, give yourself the luxury of playing around. Save up to buy the palette, find a great online tutorial, and learn a few new tricks. You are *not* a waste of your time. You are worth the effort.

LEVEL 3: EXPERT

Admittedly, I'm not at expert level yet, so I don't have a lot of ideas to share, but this doesn't mean that they don't exist—far from it. I suspect that the expert-level stuff is somewhat more personal than the easy and middle-level stuff, so it's something we each get to explore for ourselves. What might expert-level self-care look like for you? Take a moment to brainstorm some ways you can show yourself how much you matter.

~~~

These are just some of my favorite ways to show myself love without having to think too hard about it. Not having to think about it—that part's important. When I'm feeling blocked or crazy or like I'm going to slide back towards self-hate territory, I need to know what mindless stuff I can do *without feeling like it*. I need to be able to change my state quickly without having to be in the right mood first. If I just do something simple, like telling myself to take a break or put on a cute outfit, then that one little thing can be enough to interrupt the negative spiral that I was about to journey down.

If any of these ideas stood out to you, give them a try. Test them out for yourself. Make up new ones. See if actively trying to show yourself love from the outside in makes any difference in your inner life. You might find that some of these ideas really speak to you and that others don't really appeal to you; it's all fine. There is no right or wrong way to joy hunt. The only "wrong" way to do it would be to deny yourself the essential self-care you deserve. As you go, collect new ideas that are tailor-made for you to show yourself your importance.

As you explore these new practices, remember that loving yourself is the theme and filter for all of it. If you don't truly enjoy something, don't keep doing it. This isn't only about upping your quality of life or trying some fun new routine. Every action needs to be all about showing yourself love. When you clean up your room, think of it this way: "I deserve to live in a clutter-free, beautiful space, and that's what I'm giving myself right now." That sounds a lot better than "UGH, I have to clean up my crappy room again because I'm such a slob," doesn't it?

Each of these little actions should feel like unwrapping a small gift that you give to yourself. These actions are sacred, so don't give in to that little voice in your head that tempts you to turn these ideas into just another way to boss yourself around.

What are some foolproof ways you can show yourself love the next time you need it?

_____

_____

_____

_____

_____

_____

_____

_____

Is there anything that continually drains you that you could consider cutting out of your life?

_____

_____

_____

_____

_____

_____

_____

If you're up for it, list a few little loving things you want to try in the coming days:

_____

_____

_____

_____

_____

_____

_____

CHAPTER 8

THOUGHT BABYSITTING

As you begin adding some on-purpose loving actions to your life, I hope that it's blowing your mind a little bit. I hope that the idea that you might be worth loving and may be worth taking good care of is sounding more like a possibility than something to be scoffed at and pushed aside. Keep trying new things. Keep pushing boundaries. Keep tapping into your creative soul for ideas and inspiration.

In the meantime, I want to get more in-depth on a few topics with you.

As you know, in the last chapter we talked about going outside in—setting up your life in a way that inspires you to love yourself. This is a huge part of the equation. Hopefully there are subtle, practical changes you're making in your day-to-day life. I hope you are starting to catch the things in your life that drain you, and identify some specific things that light you up. But, as you can probably guess, that's only half of it. The other side of the coin is the internal stuff.

This side is admittedly a bit more involved. As you probably already know, you might be able to force yourself to get up early and go to the gym a few days in a row, but if you're *resisting internally* every step of the way, it won't be long before you're back to sleeping in every morning. We can only fake our actions for so long. At some point, we need to figure out how to make our loving actions a natural response instead of something we have to *make* ourselves do.

How? Down into our souls we go—or rather deep into our minds. To the inner world we house behind our forced smiles and lighthearted conversation. That's where real change is possible.

~~~

I have a friend who's been fighting a sticky addiction for years. I've watched him go from being apathetic about it to waging all-out war on his unwanted behavior to giving up and settling, only then to go and try to change all over again. He keeps doing the dance—deciding to change, trying as hard as he can, having a slip-up, and then feeling like a failure. So he gives up; that is, until the next time he finds the will to try again. He is exerting so much effort and making radical promises of change, but it never lasts past a couple of weeks.

I think this is in part because he has yet to make a lasting, internal belief change. He adjusts his behavior, but inside a part of him still craves his destructive habit. He needs to find a way to rip out those weeds by their roots so they stop choking out all the other potential positive growth in his life. He may keep going around and around in this little dance for years until he goes deeper and figures out what is causing this continual self-sabotage.

Looking inside ourselves is scary. It's even freakier for those of us who are not entirely confident with the quality of our internal makeup. Sometimes our brains feel more like enemies than allies, and I get that.

We can't examine our beliefs without looking at our thoughts. Learning to essentially hack your brain can be scary but also helpful—even life-changing. You may be familiar with beliefs such as *my head is broken, I cannot control the thoughts that come to me,* or *my brain just won't shut up.* Believe it or not, you *can* actually influence the kinds of thoughts that come into your head. It sounds like an insurmountable task when you don't have practice with it, but it's possible. I'm living proof of it.

This being said, I still have moments where I feel out of my mind and helpless—when I really *cannot* control what I'm thinking or feeling. That's okay. There are capable, qualified professionals who are trained in helping people like us find our way back to sanity, and there is zero shame is reaching out to a therapist, counselor, or doctor to help us along our journey. Part of loving ourselves means asking for help when we need it. Remember that.

Whether you choose to engage the services of a mental health professional in learning to control your thoughts or not, there's nothing to lose from learning how to wrangle them into submission yourself first. Can you use your thoughts to heal yourself? Can you break into your own head and make it work for you, the way it was designed to, instead of it bossing you around all day?

~~~

We are always thinking. The weird thing about thoughts is that they are usually not obvious, concrete statements in the way that talking is. You generally don't hear your brain blatantly announcing, "I look so ugly today!" in so many words. Rather, it's more of a gentle impression in which you suddenly find yourself feeling ugly. Most of the time, you don't even realize that your brain offered that thought to you and that you bought into it—you just automatically believe it.

When you become aware of your head's tendency to bully you, you can catch it in the act. I call it babysitting my thoughts.

See if you can notice your thoughts. Listen for them. Watch them closely. If they're too subtle to detect, then you can try to focus on your feelings instead. I don't know about you, but sometimes my feelings are at level-ten huge and overwhelming, which at least means they're often easier to observe than my thoughts. I can be crying on my couch for what feels like no reason, but if I take a moment to look deeper, I can usually figure it out. Maybe I start to realize that I'm crying because I'm feeling hopeless. If I gently keep asking myself where that hopeless feeling came from, I can usually trace it back to a thought I had earlier in the day. Our thoughts create our feelings, so it's good to get into a habit of noticing our feelings and then following them back to our thoughts. In doing this, we are reverse-engineering our emotions.

I want to give you some practical pointers on how to babysit your thoughts. You can learn how to become aware of the thoughts you are thinking and catch the bad guys, then escort them out of your head. Like any new habit or skill, this takes practice, but if you give yourself the time and be patient and persistent, you'll get the hang of it.

First, when I realize I'm feeling bad, I think, "Oh, crap, I feel bad." I freak out for a second, and then I start investigating. I ask myself, "What was I just thinking about? What made me feel like this?" After I ask myself this, I can usually connect the dots.

"Oh, I was just obsessing about my pores in a magnifying mirror and comparing myself to the girl in the movie I saw last night, who was totally flawless." After I've identified the culprit, I can then choose an objective, informed version of reality instead of just buying the crap that my head serves up sometimes.

"So, brain, you're telling me that because my pores are big that I should feel ugly today? Hmm…I don't know if you've actually considered this, but that chick in the movie had a whole team of professional assistants making her skin look flawless on screen. I, on the other hand, just woke up. So maybe that's not a totally fair comparison to make, yeah?"

And just like that, you can create some space between your thoughts and the truth. Again, this takes practice, and your brain's not just going to magically shut up with one telling-off, but it's so, so worth the effort.

Here's the summarized process for easy reference:

HOW TO BABYSIT & REFORM YOUR THOUGHTS

1. Begin paying attention to what you think.

2. Catch the bad thoughts as they come. You'll know they're bad if they make you feel bad.

3. Take a moment to celebrate—you got one!

4. Examine the culprit. Is it true? Where did it come from? What would you rather believe/think?

5. Replace the lie with a new statement of truth that is based in reality.

6. Get said statement tattooed. Or, you know, write it on one of those handy Post-its you've now got lying around everywhere.

Continue this rhythm of "catch and replace" and watch how things begin to change.

Whatever you do, please don't believe everything that you think. Your head is doing the best it can, but it's not always very kind, or helpful, or true. Make your head work for you by teaching it the thoughts you want it to serve up automatically instead of the stuff it naturally tends to autosuggest.

AFFIRMATIONS

When you're learning how to babysit your brain, affirmations are actually kind of helpful. You're purposefully hacking your head and reprogramming it—replacing the junk with gold. Affirmations are about as overused and cliché as you can get on the self-love path, and it took a few years (yep, years) of resistance before I broke down and gave them a shot. Turns out, they didn't suck; they actually sort of help! Before I knew it, I was putting affirmation stickies all over my room and making up new ones every day for fun.

So here you go: I present to you for your thought-babysitting pleasure my Super Official List of Affirmations. These have come from many years of playing around and seeing what I like. They're specific to me, but I hope they will inspire you to come up with some of your own.

When you read through this list, try to say some out loud. If you're in a public space, whisper them under your breath and then say them out loud when you get to a private spot. It's important to hear your own voice saying these things, because you need to notice your own internal reaction to each statement. The ones that make you cringe are the ones you believe the least, and, consequently, likely need the most. The ones that make you feel the most uncomfortable and ridiculous are probably the most important.

I am strong.

I am brilliant.

I am hot.

I value my own heart.

I have killer ideas.

I like myself.

I enjoy the human experience.

I am enough.

I am infinitely creative, I never run out of good ideas.

I am a blessing to my family.

I was born for a reason.

My existence makes the world a better place.

My smile makes people happy.

My life just keeps getting better.

No one can do it quite like me.

I'm God's favorite.

I'm my favorite, too.

My past does not define me.

I am always growing.

The world needed a me, so I was born.

~~~

You can be whoever you wanna be. For real. The only reason you won't is if you let the limiting beliefs in your own head drive. I know that's not fun to think about; it's easier to blame luck or the economy or our parents on our lack of progress. But the truth is that your happiness or lack thereof is overwhelmingly a product of what's inside your head. If you aren't where you wanna be, examine your beliefs until you find the toxic mindsets that are poisoning your efforts. Eliminate those, replace them with the truth, and see how much better you begin to feel.

Yes, you will encounter obstacles. Ones that make you feel like you can't possibly succeed. But if you can beat your brain at its own game and figure out how to get it to prop you up instead of beat you down, all of your challenges will seem more manageable. Don't let brain chatter hijack your joy, or your life.

What are some false beliefs you've been living by?

_____

_____

_____

_____

_____

_____

_____

_____

_____

_____

_____

_____

_____

_____

What are some affirmation statements that stand out to you?

_____

_____

_____

_____

_____

_____

_____

_____

_____

_____

_____

_____

_____

CHAPTER 9

MAKING SPACE FOR THE AUTHENTIC YOU

I felt so much freer in my own life when I began to actually like myself—not tolerate, put up with, or control myself, but actually enjoy the person I am. It's a radical notion. It made me feel like a rebel in a society that had taught me so well how to hate myself.

In order to learn how to love myself, I had to get to know myself first. I had to pay attention to my likes and dislikes and make peace with who I really am on a daily basis.

I swear, every day that I show up in the fullness of who I am, it feels like I am doing holy work. Every time I stand up for myself, I honor myself.

Simply being yourself is a powerful act of self-love.

I usually cringe when I hear people say, "just be yourself!" It brings back weird memories of junior high, where teachers, parents, and guidance counselors would offer up that cure-all statement to almost any issue we'd bring them. Not making friends? Oh, honey, just be yourself. Unsure what to be when you grow up? Trust yourself, it'll come. Miserable and depressed? You be you, and you'll be fine.

Being told to "just be myself" seemed pretty irrelevant for most of the issues I was struggling with, especially because, when you're a thirteen-year-old kid, you have zero clue what being yourself actually looks like. Just be myself? What does that *mean*? What else could I be? And how does this help me get a spot at the cool lunch table?

When we get a little older, we learn that, sadly, just being ourselves is not at all the answer, and in fact often equals more pain and rejection than it does acceptance. Why be yourself when you can make like a chameleon and edit your opinions to get more friends, or tone down your personality so you stop coming across as so outspoken or weird? Sometimes our life experiences tell us to hide and be small because no one could ever love the real, weird person that we actually are inside, right?

This breaks my heart. We begin our lives in a state of naive openness, just being our lovely little selves and not overthinking it, until life teaches us we are not good enough the way we are. It's no wonder so many of us have self-love issues.

It turns out that the grownups were actually right about being yourself—they were just bad at explaining what that really means.

Being ourselves simply means living from our authentic souls. My soul is my center, my very essence. It's that part of me that I'm talking about when I refer to "myself." It's letting my true, beautiful nature be seen and loved by others. It's not trying to change my essence to blend in with someone else's or to get approval.

I would never want to water my true self down, because I know that my soul is where the gold is. It's the purest place in me—that place where I am the most alive, where all my ideas flow, where all my favorite lyrics originate from. It's the part of me that makes me *me*. My life is a quest to live from my soul, my truest self.

If you're reading this and you're not sure you understand what I'm talking about, that's completely okay. I did not even *recognize* my own essence—didn't even know I had any—until my mid-twenties. It's kind of cool, actually, to begin to uncover yourself after you've already been alive for a while.

I first stumbled on my own soul essence through art-making. I noticed that some of my art (my songs, my writing, The REL Show, my DIY clothing, etc.) came from a really true, unfiltered place in me where it felt like I was just plugging in a circuit from my heart to my audiences, whereas some of it came from my desire to make something good that other people would like. No question, the authentic stuff that comes straight from my soul always brings me more long-term joy than the more external-facing stuff. My audience also tends to resonate with my most vulnerable work, and I love that so much. It makes me feel like my true nature makes sense to other people; like the more of myself I connect with and learn to express, the more of service I can be.

Being authentic just makes so much sense. It's almost like our life's purpose is just to uncover our own brilliance and then go around shining all day. I like being my true self so much that I've started building my whole life around it. I've set my life up to serve my soul, and that's been as amazing as it sounds. I love living this way. I love that I can share my true nature and people can connect with it, because it's so easy, so natural. You have your own soul essence, too, and I suggest you find out what that is and start sharing it. It doesn't matter if you make it your career or not—as long as you stay continually connected to it, you'll be living an authentic life. It will make you feel more alive, I promise. It will help you go even deeper into your true self and make it next to impossible to feel like an imposter living in your own skin.

~~~

I had an eye-opening experience with living from my true self recently. I met a woman who was a professional songwriter whose full-time job was to go around the city and write potential hit songs with other writers. She even had a song that was being pitched to Taylor Swift, which I thought was impressive. We hit it off and she suggested we try to write together. I knew my previous attempts at co-writing had been a disaster, but a few years had passed since then, and this seemed like a great way to give it another try.

She came to my house on a bright Wednesday morning with a coffee mug in one hand and a guitar in the other. We set up shop in my pretty pink soul room, where I do most of my writing, and jumped in, ready to collaborate on something amazing.

I had printed out some chords and lyric ideas (because when I Googled "how to co-write," that's what it told me to do), and we started working on one of them. She liked the melody but wanted to play around with the words. She suggested we start with the hook line and title and work from there. This was fascinating to me because it was much more structured than the way I usually write my songs, and I was excited to be getting schooled by a professional.

For the first hour, we tossed around different ideas for the hook line, which is usually the last line of the chorus, where the whole song comes to a culmination. After sixty minutes of brainstorming, we came up with something solid and moved on. We then spent the next five hours fleshing out the rest of the chorus lyrics and a first verse.

You guys. It was one of the most agonizing experiences of my life. I don't think I've ever looked at a clock more often. I don't think I've ever worked on a song's lyrics for more than an hour at a time, much less *five*. We were going about it so counter intuitively to the way that I usually write. Normally, I get on my piano and sing and play until I accidentally sing something I like, in which case I get really excited, write it down, and keep going. My view on getting blocked is this: When the going gets tough, the tough grab a snack. I have no desire to keep banging away at a song that's not flowing, because that just seems kind of dumb to me. If it's not flowing now, it might be tomorrow or next week when I come back to it, so I like to save myself the trouble and just work on it then instead.

But that's not what we were doing. What we were doing was camping out for a day on a so-so lyric idea that was going nowhere. I felt like my hands were tied; I didn't feel comfortable enough to vulnerably get on the piano and sing my heart out until something cool came out (because, admittedly, I sing a lot of lame and incoherent stuff to get to the good stuff, and that's an embarrassing process). I was also trying to be teachable and learn how the pros do it.

Apparently, what the pros do is sit around and try to come up with cool lines that rhyme. Whenever something even halfway plausible came to mind, we'd share it, and after a while I got so bored with this that I decided to just commit to mediocre to get this thing over with. This was not songwriter woman's fault; I was coming up with nothing good myself. Nothing! I stared at my blank notebook and wondered how I'd ever strung anything decent together in my life.

I realized from this experience that I write my songs on accident through the method I described earlier. I don't sit there and think, *Hmm, what should come next here? Do I want to introduce a new concept here or should I expand on what I already said?* because that process is like two people getting together to write a novel, and instead of writing the darn thing, they're busy discussing things like, "Do you think we should open it up with *Sarah came out of the woods with rosy cheeks*, or *Sarah bundled out of the woods and her cheeks glowed a rosy hue?*" Maybe that works for some people, but for me, that feels like a massive waste of time and creative resources.

Truth be told, during our writing session, I found myself wanting to sneak away to the bathroom so I could have a minute to actually think. Then maybe I could come back with the whole song done so we could call it a day.

After the songwriter left (thank God my friend was playing a show that night and I had a great excuse to finally wrap it up), I was tempted to question if my songwriting style was all wrong and if I should try to do it more like other people do it. What if I was being naive by just cranking out what's flowing? What if I should second-guess my work a little bit more?

The answer to that is obviously a giant NO. It was a painful six hours, yes, but I'm so glad I did it. I learned a lot about my creative process by trying on somebody else's. I learned that songwriting is delicious and easy and organic for me, and that there is no reason on earth to change how I write just because that's how some other musicians prefer to do it. My true essence flows effortlessly when I'm alone in my room, putting my heart to paper, and there is no reason to mess with that just to match other people's style. That would be watering myself down, and not a good career move to say the least. Like I said, your soul is where the gold is, and honoring that is how you stay true to yourself.

When I write my songs, I am living from my center and letting the gold flow out of me. It's easy, natural. That's what being myself is like—effortless, effective, and just plain smart.

You too have a beautiful, powerful essence, and you should be using it as much as you can. Experiment with different things until you find out how your soul can shine the brightest, and then do as much of that as is possible. If you can bottle up your shine and sell it, even better. People will pay good money for true, unfiltered, vulnerable soul essence, because it's a rare thing in today's cold and calculated market. I can use my authenticity to serve and connect with others. Authenticity lets me be vulnerable, it helps me connect with strangers, and it lets me love my fans in the crowd from a few hundred yards away.

What will being true to your soul allow you to accomplish?

~~~

Living from your purest center is undoubtedly *awesome*, yes, but for me it's been a clumsy road getting there. In my journey to be my full-on authentic self, I've screwed up and said and done things that I thought were me just being myself, but to my horror I've learned were actually not so great after all.

As much as I love this idea of unashamedly living an unfiltered life, it turns out that I totally *do* need a filter—otherwise I tend to say dumb things that can come across as hurtful even when I genuinely don't mean them that way. If I'm just flying on autopilot, I completely forget to smile at strangers, or hold the door for people, or ask the barista how his day is going. It's almost like being myself isn't always a good idea after all.

Now, hear me out, I'm all about letting your freak flag fly, but I also see the value in, well, growing up. Just because you've always behaved a certain way doesn't mean you have to stay that way forever. You're not a sellout if you decide to evolve. While we all have natural tendencies towards different preferences and personality traits, these are not set in stone. We can change them if we're not satisfied with them. I think there's no harm in slowly building your self-repertoire until you are happy with your tastes and habits and values. It's a big, bright world out there, and you miss out on all sorts of good stuff when you stubbornly decide it's your way or the highway on every single thing, and baby, you were born this way.

Well, I was born with natural tendencies towards depression. Should I camp out and stay in that place in a twisted commitment to be true to myself? Oh, hell, no. I'm also naturally freakishly intense, but that tendency just stresses me out and pushes people away. Even I don't like myself very much when I get overly intense, stressing out over something that doesn't have to be a huge deal. So I like to work on these parts of myself and look for new ways to get better. It's called self-improvement, and it's a part of self-care.

Self-improvement can be utterly exhausting, or it can be divinely life-giving. "Life-giving" is totally the version we're going for here. I try to view it as a hobby; I'm both the sculptor and the sculpted, and I enjoy the transformation process. It's fun and helpful to me because I am doing it from a place of strength and compassion towards myself. I try not to stress out or beat myself up after recognizing yet another part of myself that's not working. On the contrary; I usually get excited, ready and eager to infuse more energy into that area of my life. I do this knowing that I am not inherently flawed. I'm not an endless self-help project that never stays fixed. I know my core, my soul, has been handcrafted by God himself, and he and I like me very much.

Need some ideas on how to amp up the authenticity in your life? You're in luck, because I've got some for ya.

WEAR WHAT YOU WANT.

Wear what *you* want! It's fine to let culture and trends influence your tastes, but it's kinda lame to buy and wear something you don't love just because you think you're supposed to. Fill your closet with clothes that make you delighted to get dressed every morning, and go out into the world with your head held high no matter how in or out of style your badass outfit is and no matter where you bought it.

I've found that an outfit is made cool by how you wear it rather than by what the individual pieces actually are. By "how," I mean your confidence when you walk into a room—your posture, your eye contact—the fact that you know you are totally owning your look. Don't sheepishly go about your day, searching for subconscious permission to dress the way you want. Own it.

I was hanging with some of my friends a while back and a local coffee house came up. It's a cool space—they sell delicious, handcrafted coffees in a beautiful warehouse setting, play hipster music, and serve biscuits on wooden planks. The girls were discussing how they always feel self-conscious at that particular coffee shop because everyone always looks so put together and so much cooler than them.

I knew better than to say it, but I had never felt that way when I went there. I hadn't really given it that much thought; I knew I looked awesome and I knew I deserved a spot at the community coffee table just because I'm human. It bums me out that such wonderful, kickass women like my friends would feel anything less than like rockstars anywhere they go. I want them to walk into a room focusing on the people they're about to meet and the impact they're about to have on the world, not whether their outfit meets the bar or not.

If you have a love-hate (mostly hate) relationship with your wardrobe, I'd encourage you to spend some time figuring out what makes you feel good and then going the distance to wear those things. Skinny jeans even if you're not a 5' 11" Victoria's Secret model? Sweet. Breezy, bold prints and tons of jewelry and scarves? Awesome. All black, 365 days of the year? Do it.

Whatever you're wearing, commit to it, love it, and feel good in it.

FOR GOD'S SAKE, USE YOUR REAL VOICE!

Not the sweet, peppy one you use at work while sucking up to your boss or while trying to sound nice on the phone. In an attempt to come across as kind and caring to cashiers, strangers, or even fans, I often put on my ultra-sweet voice, which is about two octaves higher than my actual voice. I sound like a timid nine-year-old (but at least I sound nice, right?!) The intentions behind this impulse are totally good, but let's stop sounding like a bunch of church mice when interacting with society. Most women I know do this, and definitely a handful of dudes, too.

Let's not forget that we can be kind and pleasant without coming across as timid and small. We should allow ourselves to be kind, gentle, and loving while also using our real voices when greeting strangers, or talking to customer service reps, or chatting with long-lost friends.

Show up in the fullness of who you are.

STOP WORRYING ABOUT WHAT YOUR PARENTS THINK OF YOU.

This is a big one. Something about the connection we have with our parents makes their opinions (real or imagined) especially hard to shake. Most of us had childhoods that celebrated fitting in and keeping the peace, not blazing our own trails. We can make serious progress in our lives only to come home for Christmas and find we're still craving validation from the people who raised us.

I love my parents, but I can't let their hopes and expectations for me mess with my own. I think there may come a time in everyone's life where they have to take a step back and reevaluate the dynamic they have with their parents. This is not to be confused with questioning the relationship, or growing distant, although I suppose that could be a part of the process, as well. It's just healthy to take some time practicing being your true self, away from the people who think they already know everything there is to know about you.

Most people I know have a really strong fear of disappointing their parents or letting them down in some way, and their parents' opinions matter a disproportionate amount to them. If you notice this in your life, begin experimenting with cultivating a sense of independence from your parents' opinions and desires. I don't want to live under the metaphorical watchful eye of my mom and dad for the next forty years, because this will only hold me back. It will keep me in fear, guessing what their response to my next move will be. The only way I know to combat this is to keep making decisions for myself rather than for them.

When my band released "Now You Know"—our first song that featured explicit lyrics, among other things—it was a little scary for me. I stayed awake at night wondering what my parents' reaction would be. But I went for it anyway. And you know what? My dad was like "I'm so proud of you!" and my mom didn't even catch the adult words because English is her second language. Basically, it was no big deal.

Taking bold steps in the complete opposite direction of what your parents would choose for you can be very liberating, and a healthy way to create some new patterns—as long as those steps serve you and your authentic soul. Try it.

ACTUALLY, STOP WORRYING WHAT ALL OF US THINK OF YOU.

Something wonderful happens when you stop imagining what people are thinking about you. Suddenly, a whole lot of headspace opens up when you're not wondering how you come across to the rest of the world. As a musician, I've had plenty of practice with not internalizing other people's opinions of me, and I've realized I can't afford to care. I don't have the time or mental energy to wonder how everyone feels about me.

There have been situations where haters have gone out of their way to let me know their opinions about me, and usually, seriously considering what they have to say is of no real value to me. I'm not going to change based on their hate speech. If I have no intention of doing something with their critique, then I'm better off just ignoring it in the first place. And I practice that. I don't go around reading online comments about myself unless I know it's a hater-free zone, like my Patreon page. It takes a lot of discipline, but I don't read mean-spirited articles about the band, either. It's not good for my heart.

All this practice has translated into other parts of my life, too, where I don't find myself wondering what people are thinking of me nearly as often as I used to. You can practice that, as well, and intentionally stop yourself when you begin to wonder what others are thinking of you (Remember thought babysitting? This is it!) Do your best to be kind and considerate and all that, but don't be super concerned with other people's opinions. Be brave and inspire people to be themselves by boldly being yourself, and you will evoke a chain reaction of badass authenticity.

WANT WHAT YOU HAVE.

Another way of being yourself is to want what you have. Actively want to be the person you already are. Be happy with what you have. I can already hear you thinking, "Won't this make me lazy, complacent, and keep me stuck where I am instead of improving?" No, darling. It will make you shine, and I promise that your soul's desires will never be silenced by self-love; they will only grow.

This means taking a neutral part of yourself and deciding it's your new favorite thing. Straight hair? Decide to love it. Curly hair? Embrace it, and spend time learning how to rock it. Are you a good listener? That's amazing! Own that skill, because a lot of us don't have it (and wish we did).

Whatever we're good at, we should let ourselves enjoy that instead of wishing for the opposite. There are other people who would give anything to look or think or create like you, and they'd probably be mad to hear that you're not even enjoying it because you're wishing you had something else!

I've definitely had to do this in my own life with my introversion. I am inherently, helplessly introverted—I don't like being with a lot of people for too long. Rather than fight this, I actively let myself love this part of myself. My dad is a strong introvert, too, and I feel proud to so clearly be his daughter. I love the joy that I feel while unwinding all by myself, taking a hot shower after a chaotic show, or listening to an audiobook after working and dreaming all day. This is a great part of myself, and I have no intention of changing it even though I spend large parts of my life on a stage.

I also love obnoxiously overproduced pop music. I have more Britney Spears records than any other artist. I am probably *supposed* to like hardcore and alternative music, since that's the kind of scene my band most often circles. But I'm not gonna mess with my natural inclination towards pop music, because I enjoy it so much. I'm fine with this. If you like something, let yourself like it, even if it's unexpected or maybe even uncool.

This self-acceptance practice goes way beyond just enjoying physical features, personality traits, or preferences. Wanting what you have applies to the life you have, too. I see city people dreaming of organic gardens and chicken coops and rural people fantasizing about high rises and endless coffee shops to choose from. If you want another life, start working on going out and getting it, but if that's not feasible for one reason or another, then make peace with the life you already have—the one that other people are currently dreaming about.

This is how happy people embrace their lives and stay enthusiastic about their place in the world. They're content because they've decided that they want the lives they have! Be where you are so you can be who you are. Love who you're with, and this includes yourself.

~~~

When I began honoring my authentic soul essence, I couldn't help but fall in love with other people's, as well. What a mind-blowing concept it is to realize that everyone else has an inner life as huge and complex as your own; that every single person walking past you has their own agendas, their own fears, their own preferences, and their own *life*. To them, you're just a passerby, a blurry object walking towards them and just as quickly fading out of their life.

But it doesn't have to be so impersonal. We don't have to view other people only in direct correlation to how they affect our own world. Once you begin to believe in your own value, you may find yourself seeing the value in others more easily. Self-love can't be contained; it spills out as love for all of humankind.

I worked a short stint at Burger King when I was 14. I ran the cash register and operated the fancy drive-through headset. I cleaned the lobby and scarfed down frozen chunks of cookie dough from the freezer in the back in between customers.

I was privy to a special luxury of regular human interaction in that it was my job to take orders. I began noticing a few things as I did this. People never looked at me, instead always at the menu that hung above and behind my head or leafing through their wallet for cash or demanding a decision from their distracted children. It was clear that their minds were usually just on one thing: getting through this transaction in a way that got them their food as quickly as possible—it isn't called fast food for nothing. Sometimes, old people would speak too slowly, looking up at the menu and taking their sweet time to ask their spouse what they had last time and what they wanted this time, annoying myself as well as the people behind them with their complete disregard for a busy lunch rush.

I began realizing through these predictable interactions that customers could have a huge influence on the quality of my day. Every once in a great while, one of these transactions would turn into something a little bit more than barking out an order at me. It would evolve into a true human connection in which the customer would see me as an actual person instead of just a cog in their lunchtime machine. They would look at me when ordering, remember their manners, and somehow make me feel like they *saw* me. When you work behind a counter, you generally feel more machine than human, because that's how people tend to treat you. You could be a computer for all they care; they just want to get what they came for in the fastest and most painless way possible.

I started to play around with this, seeing if there was something I could do to get the customer to remember I was human. I'd do my best to see *them* as a person, rather than just a customer in my busy day. I'd look them in the eye and speak purposefully, doing my best to let them know I cared about their experience, that I cared about *them*. This wasn't because I gave a rip about building Burger King's empire with my stellar customer service, but because I knew that there was an opportunity for an actual emotional exchange, and I wanted to let people know I was willing. *I'm willing to make this about more than chicken nuggets, if you are. I am kind, I am loving, and you deserve love.*

Most people missed it, of course, because they never looked up long enough to notice. Even if they had, I'm sure a lot of people didn't particularly want to engage with me; they were stuck in their own heads and didn't exactly come to BK for a moment of deep connection with the cashier.

My days as a fast food employee taught me a good deal about humanity. I promised myself to be a good person, a good customer when it came to be my turn, and to try to treat the person behind the counter with respect whenever possible.

It's not easy. Even though I have every intention to be mindful about that, many times I shuffle through it, lost in my own thoughts, going through the transaction as if in a trance. I'm often thinking *I know you want me to hurry up and get out of here, don't worry, I'll be easy and get this over with as soon as possible.* I often default to invisibility rather than making a positive impression on someone. I feel embarrassed to be a consumer rather than a server and try to minimize the awkwardness by making myself smaller in the moment. Of course, by doing this, I am reducing the quality of our interaction, and love is the casualty.

Still, I try to remember that with every possibility for human interaction there is also possibility for human connection. I wish everyone in the world knew this and lived by it. All the other people I encounter throughout my day have a whole universe of thoughts inside of themselves. I can play an active role in making their day better, even if it's hard sometimes, and even if I'm not always met with openness and love in return. I still try to create that connection whenever possible. I try to remember to show up in life authentically, as *me*, and to give others full room to show up as themselves, too. That's what this is all about. When we learn how to love ourselves, we can all freely *be* ourselves.

~~~

Are there any areas of your life that aren't feeling good because you're not being true to yourself? Are there any people or situations that you continually water yourself down around or in?

_____

_____

_____

_____

_____

_____

What do you suspect are some amazing aspects of your true soul essence? (For example, "I believe I'm someone who knows how to emotionally connect with and inspire other people," or "I think I might be really good at making others feel heard," or even "I suspect that I am a fierce badass!")

_____

_____

_____

_____

_____

What are some killer ways you could amp up the authenticity in your life?

_____

_____

_____

_____

_____

_____

CHAPTER 10

UNLEASHING YOUR SELF-EXPRESSION THROUGH CREATIVITY

One of the clearest signs that I am living from my true self is that I can't stop making stuff. It's like creative content spills out of me; self-being inspires self-expression.

Our souls are begging to share themselves. When you let your true self show, you're giving the people around you the permission to do the same. When you express yourself in authentic ways, it inspires others. Isn't that wonderful? Conversely, when you hold back, everybody suffers, including you.

We're all creative, and we are all constantly creating, even if our art is (only) our lives. Our goal should be to keep teasing out every drop of creativity and self-expression that lives within us. Soul-expression is one of my favorite parts of being human. It's one of those things that lights me up and makes my life worth living. Plus, I don't need a lot of special equipment or a degree or a staff of 20 to turn an idea living in my heart into a real, live thing.

I wonder if everybody enjoys being creative as much as I do. (Do you?) It is such a huge source of bliss for me, and I'm reminded of this every time I work on something that I really love. In school, I was given the impression that you were either artistic or you weren't (if you weren't, it meant you were into sports/math/science; things that still require constant creativity, but weren't regarded as "creative" pursuits). Contrary to this, this instinct to create and express seems so primal to me that I can't imagine that a huge chunk of the population is somehow born without it.

If, like me, you enjoy using your creativity, I think you should do it as much as you can. If you like playing guitar, invest in that; save up to buy the equipment you need and spend time on it. If you're curious about jewelry-making, then dig into that; develop your craft and make it a big part of your life. If you're passionate about studying astrophysics, then find fun, creative ways to make your learning process uniquely yours! There really aren't many deeper joys in life than finding your favorite ways to express yourself, whether or not that means sharing your self-expression with the world through a career.

I want to challenge you to get hopelessly lost in the art you make. Go down for days and come out on the other side with scrapes and bruises—and a masterpiece.

I'm convinced that making stuff and using your creative heart is one of the most rewarding ways to live. Is there any better way to spend your time, your life? Besides being with people you love, I can't think of a better payoff on a time investment. Even if you spend hours working on something and it never blooms into the vision you had for it, just the joy of working on something often makes it worth it. I get so much energy from writing a song I love that, regardless of whether it makes it on the record or not, the process and the time I spend working on it is valuable in and of itself. Seeing art this way helps take away some of the fear of "What if no one *gets* this?" No matter. The idea needed to be born, and the mere creation of it is rewarding on its own.

My years of enjoying my own creativity have taught me a few things, and I've been trying to pay attention along the way. Where do I feel the most inspired? What can I do to make the process as satisfying as possible? I've been asking myself questions and taking mental notes for easy reference. Here's what I've got so far:

I only like to make things when I feel inspired. I don't like to "push through" artistic blocks. If the idea's gonna come, it'll come when it's ready.

I prefer to make things in my home, or at least in a pretty environment. Travel also sparks creativity.

Once I get the ball rolling, it feels effortless, and the thing sort of makes itself.

I like to be alone and uninterrupted. Do *not* walk in on me mid-creation!

I generally like my creation when I've first made it. When I revisit it the next day, I find out if it's actually good or not.

My creative process is something like going down into a deep, dark cave, passing through doorways and hallways that turn off as I go, and barreling straight through until I reach the center. In the deepest, darkest center of the cave, I am unreachable and untouchable by the outside world, completely immersed in the process. This is how I can get lost for hours in my work, ignoring hunger pains and text messages alike.

The deeper I venture into my artistic cave, the purer the art I create there; I can't hear the expectations of my management team or my audience or even the old self-hating voices in my own head when I'm neck-deep in my creative process. This is that magic sweet spot that artists before me have referred to as "flow," and this experience of flow is one of the ultimate payoffs for being creative.

Do everything you can to make this journey to the center of your creative flow on a regular basis.

I've also had to learn some mental hacks that help me get to that state of flow a little more quickly and stay there a little more effortlessly. By listening to my creative tendencies, I've realized that there are certain things that work for me and certain things that can kill my buzz in seconds. It's been helpful for me to be observant of my own unique creative process. That way, I can make space for myself (literally and figuratively) in order to create as joyfully as possible. Here are some of my guidelines for creativity. Feel free to adapt them to your own process!

IF IT FEELS HOT, DO IT, AND DO IT NOW.

If you're feeling inspired, go there. Even if it's a weekend and you had planned on resting instead of working on your project, go where your creativity is taking you. Even if it's late and you really should get to bed. Even if you have to rearrange your whole day around a sporadic strike of inspiration. If your juices are flowing, if gold is brewing, take advantage of that. Don't push your ideas back down and tell them to come back later. They won't.

MAKE THINGS WITH AS LITTLE FANFARE AS POSSIBLE.

You don't have to tell your mom and the mailman and your neighbor's dog what you're working on. "So what's next?" everyone wants to know. Don't tell them. I find that I exponentially prefer just jumping in with minimum expectations or planning and just going for it. That way, I get to surprise myself after it's finished, like "Oh, look, you just wrote a song!" rather than "Okay, girl, I need you to write this song."

The approach I take matters, and this one serves me well. There's nothing better than sharing something you've just made with another human being, but I'm learning that I can't do that until it's actually finished—like, all the way. The novelty of getting to tell people "I wrote a book!" instead of "I'm writing a book!" makes all the difference for me. Once it's out in the open and people know I'm working on something, it's just not fun for me anymore, and I move onto the next shiny new project.

SET THE MOOD.

While I admire people who can write albums on the road or compose blog posts on the train, that's usually not my thing. I like to work in pretty, well-lit places, with candles burning and tea in my favorite mug. I like to be completely alone so no one can hear me or ask me what I'm working on. Being interrupted from my state of flow feels like someone dragging me out of bed while in the middle of a deep sleep. "Just five more minutes!" I beg of the rude soul who dares interrupt my process. Of course, inspiration strikes at some really inconvenient times, and I've learned I have to honor her, regardless of the timing or environment. If I ignore her and ask her to please come back later when the timing is better for me, I'll usually lose her.

IT'S OKAY TO GRAZE.

I like working on multiple creative endeavors at once, bouncing from project to project depending on what I'm feeling. I'll work on something until I get stuck or bored with it, and I like having something else to pick up in its stead. Even within one project, I love getting multiple plates spinning all at once, choosing to work on inspired pieces rather than completing one part and moving on to the next. This way, I can keep everything feeling authentic and everything made with love. It also prevents me from having to develop strict creative disciplines and properly organize my thoughts, but I choose to overlook those small flaws in favor of doing work in a way that I enjoy.

LET IT BE EASY.

This is so good, and so true. It can literally be as easy as you want it to be. You *could* lock yourself in your closet and bang your head against the wall and vow to not come out until you have the next greatest symphony ever written in hand, or you could simply...let it flow. You could spend months in a state of anxiety and ignore all your relationships and drive yourself into a depressed state until you emerge with a masterpiece, or you could joyfully approach your work one inspired moment at a time.

Creating doesn't have to make us crazy (unless we want it to). Let it flow. If it's not flowing, take a break to regroup. Grab a snack, go watch a movie. Sometimes, no matter how ideal the environment or how perfect your team, it just won't come to you. I've actually found that sometimes, having everything just right and ready to go can cause me to overanalyze, freak out, and expect too much. I have to let it be easy. If nothing's coming to me, I back off and browse blog posts or do dishes until I feel like making something again. I've learned that not having the perfect setting or tools is exactly what my creativity needs to take the pressure off at times, and then I just let it do its thing.

I want to invite you to become a student of your own creativity. Look out for your patterns, and take note of when you're flowing and when you're feeling blocked. You can set your life up to make it easier to put yourself into that state of creative bliss as often as you'd like.

SHARING YOUR ART IS SCARY—BUT THAT'S OKAY.

After you've made something your soul is proud of, you really ought to consider sharing it with the rest of us. It's one of the most personal things a person can do, therefore making it one of the most courageous. And I'm talking about genuine art, from one human heart to another, not the manufactured kind that's created primarily for profit. A lot of people make art with the sole intention of selling it, which can pollute the process. Creating with only the end in mind can suck a lot of the life out of your creative identity.

If you have an idea or a skill that you are thinking about sharing, I want to suggest—no, flat out insist—that you stop holding out on us. Seriously, we need what you've got. You making your thing and sharing it with the world is one of the primary reasons that *you* were even created in the first place.

Trust me, I'm familiar with the head games; I know how easy it is to talk yourself out of this. When you put something out there into the world, it *will* be criticized and/or ignored. This sucks so much. My heart still flinches when I think about the ways people have and haven't responded to my art over the years. It's a really vulnerable thing to make something and share it, knowing that I am swinging the door to criticism wide open. I am allowing for the possibility that I'll release something wonderful into the world and that no one will appreciate it. I'm also creating the possibility of sharing something that I will dislike or disagree with later on in my life, and it's hard knowing that I might not always be doing my very best work. When I start to go down that mental spiral, I have a few one-liners that I like to run through my head:

Some is better than none.

It is so important for me to remember that reaching 70% of my vision is better than reaching zero percent of perfection. We artists are tough on ourselves; we see the glaring holes in our creative work, and we like to point them out to ourselves before others can. There are so many amazing ideas and projects sitting on the shelves of my brain, waiting to see the light of day. And you know what? I may never share them, because they are imperfect, incomplete, and I simply don't know what to do with some of them. But if I ever want to turn them into living, breathing, human art, I will have to take them off the shelf, one at a time, and make peace with the idea of releasing imperfect pieces. If I waited until every project was dead-on before I shared it, there would be no projects to speak of.

The dumbass punks who make cruel comments about your art online are just lonely loser guys sitting in their moms' basements.

I know this for a fact, because I know that no one who is actually living their life with intention and attempting to share their heart with others would have the time to sit around and troll. The act of sharing your art is humbling and humanizing; it causes you to have tremendous grace for everyone else in the same boat as you. So if someone is cutting down your work in a mean-spirited (read: non-constructive) way, learn to not give them the time of day. They are not "your people," and they are not worth an ounce of your energy—pity, maybe, but not energy. Look the other way, and go back to doing what you do best: creating, and getting lost in the joy of it.

Vulnerability is irresistible.

You need to believe that the general population is rooting for you. Most people are good, kindhearted individuals who have no interest in watching you fail. We are on your side, and when we see you putting yourself out there, we are inspired by your courage, and we are cheering for you. Your humanity, your imperfections: they only make us love you more. This is something I try to remember every time I walk on stage—most of the audience is not waiting for me to screw up. I get up there and do what I do, and I don't spend a lot of time asking myself what the crowd thinks about that. I try to get as vulnerable as I can on stage, because I know that it gives people a chance to connect with me, and once that's accomplished, then game over. I've got them in the palm of my hand. Even if I get off key, or trip up on stage, they will be more likely to sympathize with me than smirk and cut me down. The same is true for you. Practice public vulnerability.

You're more brilliant/talented/creative than you give yourself credit for.

You are used to yourself, so you probably no longer recognize just how special you are. But don't write yourself off, thinking, "Oh everybody knows this", or "Anybody could do this". That simply isn't true. I'm constantly amazed by people who tell me I helped them with such-and-such when I said this-and-this on my podcast or in a lyric. It surprises me because it strikes me as so obvious, as it has already been embedded in my belief system. You have gifts and ideas that seem so natural to you that you don't even know how wonderful they are. I dare you to share them and find out. Just because something is second nature to you doesn't mean the general population is in the same place. Something can be kind of boring to you but fascinating to other people. My skills and my views and my way of doing things are unique to me, and fresh to the world. I can't devalue myself just because I strike myself as ordinary.

You will wonder if your work sucks.

I want to let you in on a secret about the creative process; one that people rarely talk about. Most people think creating is a simple, one-step thing: You just make stuff. But it isn't. It's a two-step thing. Step one is indeed called "Create," but step two always follows, though nobody wants to admit it. Step two is called "This Sucks." It almost always sneaks in after Create. I can't remember making anything I love without hearing "This Sucks" come through a little while later. The question isn't if you'll hear that voice, it's a matter of how long you can go on creating without listening to it. That's our job: to create and ignore the voice inside telling us how much this sucks.

~~~

Share your art. Give some of it away for free, trade some of it for something else valuable to you, and most certainly sell it for money if it feels right. But be prepared that when money gets involved, a whole new level of weirdness can come with it. Because so much digital content costs a one-time fee to create but costs nothing at all to share online, as artists, we can't hide behind these costs like we used to. It feels more comfortable to sell a physical album for $9.99 than to sell the same album as mp3s for the same price. It's hard for us to ask our fans to pay for something that appears to be *pure profit*. It brings up issues of worthiness, like, "Will you love my creation enough to pay for it even when it is a naked, stripped, digital thing? Will my creativity alone be enough to hold your attention?"

Things also start getting a little weird when you begin making things for other people who are waiting for it and counting on your creative efforts. I went a little crazy while writing our second record, *Icon For Hire*, because I couldn't stop thinking of the fans who were expecting it. We wrote it in the dead of winter while living in the tiny, uninspiring town of Decatur, and I think I spent more time crying than actually writing songs. It was all wrong for me—the guys at the label kept asking to hear the tracks, the fans all knew we were writing, and there were too many people depending on the stuff coming out of my head. It's no fun to sit at a piano, see your record label president's face in your mind's eye, and ask yourself what that 50-year-old dude will think of what you're about to write. It took a lot of the joy out of the process, and I psyched myself out—I approached it anxiously and mechanically rather than letting it be easy and letting it flow. By the end of that, I was tired, and I didn't want to write another song for years.

I vowed to make that the last time I turned something as wonderful as making music into a lackluster discipline.

Writing that album was really hard, yes, but it was also filled with these moments of amazement. I'd write a bridge in my piano room and sing it back to Shawn and Adam. They'd freak out and confirm what I knew all along: *This shit is gold.* I couldn't wait for other people to hear it. We had so many moments recording in the studio on Pico Boulevard in Los Angeles when Shawn and our producer Mike Green would write a riff or a cool synth piece and we would all be convinced it was the most amazing thing ever written. It felt like we were blazing our own trail, making history while being relentlessly authentic, making what we loved and sharing that with the world.

I assumed it was simple; we were putting so much love and passion into these songs, so surely the world would hear that when they listened! Surely the music industry would be changed forever by our contribution! Surely we would look back, counting our checks and Rolexes and telling *Rolling Stone*, "We knew it all along. We just did what was in our hearts, man, and people can feel that."

Back to reality. It was a sobering lesson for me when our second album didn't win us Grammys and the admiration of the whole music industry. The album didn't do poorly by any means, but it was a small stone cast into a big pond (and, ya know, our label didn't put any money into promoting it or making music videos for it. So that might've hurt us a little). We put a lot of love and heart into our first album, *Scripted*, but I felt like I had really stepped up my vulnerability on the second one. I thought that would automatically translate into clear-cut success and that our efforts would be rewarded with tangible, measurable results. In reality, it did about as well as our first album. (I think. The label stopped sending us sales reports when we began voicing our concerns over some of their practices.)

I wish that second record would have done mind-blowingly well if only to confirm what I've always hoped is true: *If you make art that you love, others will love it, too.* The more you put in, the more you'll get out. I have always believed that taking risks and staying true to yourself pays off, that the rest of the world will be attracted to the authenticity and courage in your project, and reward you.

I was half-right. Yes, taking risks and staying true to yourself pays off, but not in the way I'd expected. Making something you love does not always translate to world-renowned success. I've heard other musicians talk about this, and you probably have, too. They put out a killer first record, it does amazing, and then you hear them talking to interviewers about the second record, the one that's about to be released. They have a twinkle in their eye, a fearlessness you haven't seen in them before, and they're telling the magazine that this new record is some of the best stuff they've ever written and that they're really proud of it. Then the record comes out and, to be honest, it just kind of sucks. It has none of the awesome elements of the first record, and none of the fans are that into it. The album sells so-so, and the band falls into obscurity.

I always thought those musicians were stupid. I thought, "If your first record was awesome, just give us another version of that." But that is being completely unfair; that's treating those musicians like a machine and not considering how they feel about it. Because I know that making something you love pays off in a big way, regardless of if other people love it. Making something you love means that you will have a record (or a painting, or a book) that makes you happy every time you encounter it. That feels like home. Even now, when I listen to our songs (which isn't often, because when you play those songs live every night you're not exactly itching to hear them again), I'm blown away by how much I love them. It feels like someone wrote an album just for me, with all the elements and lyrics that mean a whole freaking lot to me. That's not to say it's all perfect or that I don't see some things we could have done differently, but I can say that it is extremely special to me, and I'm genuinely proud of it. I could share that art with anyone on the planet and be confident they are getting the real picture of what kind of musician and writer and soul that I was at that time in my life.

To me, that's success. That beats writing a crappy, heartless song with radio appeal any day. In a perfect world, people would write songs they love and believe in *and* they'd all become hits. For me, a lot of the music that the general public seems to enjoy does not light my fire; I have no business trying to write a song about leaving my panties at the party or telling you to turn up the beat when I walk into the club. That is not why I became an artist. What I'm saying is, you have to really love the stuff you make. You have to be willing to live with it for the rest of your life. Once a song does well, you have to sing that thing live night after night for thousands of nights, and if you didn't love it begin with…you're screwed. At the same time, I can't blame musicians who write songs like those one bit. I want them to do what makes them happy, not what makes me happy. You've got to live your creative truth—as long as you've found a way to do that, whatever success you receive is just frosting.

Do you think of yourself as a creative person? Is your creative heart being regularly expressed in your life?

_____

_____

_____

_____

_____

_____

_____

_____

_____

Where do you feel the most creative? Who are you with, and what are you making?

_____

_____

_____

_____

_____

_____

Do you have a specific creative process? Are there any habits that seem to affect your inspiration levels?

_____

_____

_____

_____

_____

_____

_____

CHAPTER 11

DISCOVERING YOUR UNIQUE SELF-IMAGE

I was lying in my bed, curled up under the covers, feeling warm and cozy. It was one of those rare and precious mornings where I had nowhere to be, no plane to catch, and no conference call to dial in to. So I took a moment to have a moment.

Moments rock, in case you didn't know, and the surest way to have one is to just give yourself one.

That's what I did that morning. I let myself look for and be grateful for all the awesome things that were currently going right in my life. I noticed the sunshine seeping through the cracks in the blinds. I thought about my fridge full of European cheese and not-from-concentrate orange juice. I glanced over at my pretty pink bathrobe and thought about how excited I was to crank Sia's latest release and take a hot shower that morning.

After a minute or two of this, I was more than ready to get up and start my day. But before I ripped the sheets off and started taking things on, I took another moment to be thankful for *me*. Not the "Thank you God that I'm still alive and I don't have cancer" obvious stuff, but rather an intentional moment of appreciation for everything I enjoy about myself.

If you've never tried this, I should tell you that it's not especially easy. I never naturally hear myself thinking, "Damn, my hair is awesome and I have a killer personality and everyone wants to be friends with me and I'm just so freaking fabulous!" I doubt anybody has it that easy. No one has (much less wakes up with) a pre-installed cheerleader inside their own head telling them how very wonderful they are. What most of us *do* have is a loud, obnoxious critic that lies in wait at all times, ready to read off The List of everything we did wrong yesterday, how stupid we sounded talking to that dude, how many days it's been since we've worked out, and how horrible we are with our money and on and on. That stuff? *That's* what comes easy.

So, lying in bed that morning, it took me a minute, but slowly, carefully, a few nice thoughts began to surface. I opened them gently and with great care, like birthday presents.

I love how I'm prioritizing my own happiness.

I feel hot and free today.

Yes: I'm remembering to love myself this morning!

When a few good feelings start surfacing, just stop for a second and pause there. Take up the whole space of that moment, immerse yourself in that feeling, stay with it. Let it all be very easy, gentle. Remember artistic flow? This is the same concept, just applied slightly differently. You can't force this self-love stuff, so don't boss yourself around saying stuff like, "Stay with this moment, dammit! What are you doing, stop getting distracted!" Just chill. Focus on your breathing, on your heartbeat, on your smile. This is your moment, and it may be the only one you remember to give yourself all day long.

When you're there, right in the middle of your moment, try playing around with what *feels amazing*. Feeling amazing is the whole point of moments, and pausing to really take in those feelings means you'll really get your moment's worth. Are you excited? Feel that. Are you making memories with people you love? Soak in the love all around you. Are you proud of yourself? Breath into that sensation.

The way you feel is so very important. Most people don't care very much about how they feel, and I'm willing to bet you haven't given your feelings a lot of weight in your life. Most of us treat our feelings as trivial or as an afterthought, not a central factor when living our lives or making decisions. Women seem to be especially "good" at this. I know that, as a woman, I've mastered the skill of completely ignoring and disregarding my feelings in order to not come across as annoying to all the dudes I work with. My natural tendency is to think, "Feelings are illogical, impractical—something to be overcome rather than honored. If I'm going to win in a male-dominated industry, I can't afford to give my feelings the time of day. Women are crazy people, their hormones dictate their mood and make them hypersensitive, whiny little things. No, thanks."

This toxic thinking got so bad that I even read books about how to live beyond your feelings. I guess I thought that on the other side of feeling mastery was a magical land awaiting me, full of logic and reason, clear thinking and responsible decisions. Because that all sounded real nice.

It took me a couple of years—and more than a few testosterone-dominated tours where our home-on-wheels smelled like our bassist's sweaty shoes and Little Caesar's pizza—to come to the conclusion that my life needed to be hearing *more* from my feelings, not less. My feelings were trying to tell me something, and I did myself no favors by pretending they didn't exist. I've realized that my feelings and intuition aren't the enemy here; rather, they're one of my biggest assets. So I listen to them[3].

Back to my moment. Lying in bed, doing my best to shower myself in kind thoughts and gratitude, I thought yet again about my self-

---

[3]Danielle LaPorte's *The Desire Map* played a central role in my growth of honoring my feelings. I can't recommend it highly enough.

image. I closed my eyes and tried for the millionth time to "see" myself. Sometimes this works, sometimes it doesn't. I don't really have this part figured out yet, but I do know that it's very important; maybe even the most important. My self-image influences everything I do, but it is so abstract and so deeply ingrained in my psyche that I can never quite see it for what it really is.

Here's what I do know, though: My self-image affects *absolutely everything.* I've thought long and hard of ways to fix it or outsmart it. I imagine that if only I could see it more clearly, I could pinpoint what is "wrong" with it and go to work on making it better. But self-image isn't like that. It's implanted in you, buried so deep within you would never know it's there unless you first knew to look for it.

Put simply, your self-image is like a selfie that is embedded deep in your soul. It's how you view yourself in the deepest, most honest, unfiltered sense. It is *not* a list of adjectives that describe yourself ("I'm a well-rounded, confident artist who is doing her best to make the world better"), and it's not even your opinion of yourself ("I'm doing all right; I have a ton of issues but I think I'm growing.") It is so, so much deeper than that. And it seeps into everything. Your posture, your tone of voice, your subtle facial expressions, the amount of eye contact you make. Self-image affects all of it. It runs the show.

At the risk of sounding kinda weird, the only way I've found to observe an up-to-date picture of my self-image is to imagine myself inside my head, behind my face, and note what I believe my face looks like. I can make (what I believe to be) accurate conclusions about my self-image by observing my countenance from the inside out. What my face actually looks like is not the point, but rather how I view it from backstage. Like I said, it's weird.

Most often, when I take my self-image inventory, I get the same answer: I see myself as young, naive, wide-eyed, and wanting too much from life. I assume others think I'm critical, and I'm afraid that maybe I am. I feel misunderstood, but I also feel special, and I feel like *Amy*—which is what I was called for the first 15 years of my life. It's what my family still calls me. I picture myself as a four-year-old in Sweden, with my bluntly cut blonde hair and fat cheeks. I understand that girl's heart; it is one and the same as mine. Sometimes seeing myself from that point of view helps me to remember who I am at my core, and it makes me have compassion for myself.

As you probably noticed, my default self-image as I've described isn't particularly awesome. I'm working every day to change this; to gently alter the way I perceive myself and the way I assume that the world sees me. In doing so I like to "check in" with myself regularly; I do this partly to see where I'm at, but mostly to make a conscious effort to change. I don't want to feel young, silly, naive. I want to feel hot, badass, brilliant…like (insert famous gorgeous woman of the moment here—most of us will probably go with Angelina Jolie.) It takes just a second of imagining feeling this way and I can observe the way I hold my eyes and mouth starting to change. My gaze gets sexier, like I've got perfectly applied false lashes and cateye liner decking me out. My lips curl up into a hint of a smirk—*I know something you don't know*—and I start to feel powerful. Sure, it may be a bit much, but it's a perfect balance to my natural feelings of smallness. The way I see it, *you can never feel too good about yourself.*

The way you think your face looks matters. Do you think your eyes are kind, soft, inviting? Or do you assume no one notices you so you don't give other people a chance by refusing to make eye contact? Do you imagine your face to be pretty? Is there ever a time you imagine being attractive? How you think you look will totally affect how you actually look and act. Start imagining that you might be the most gorgeous thing ever. And a heads up—we're going *deep* on this subject in the next chapter.

We perceive ourselves the way we believe everyone else perceives us.

The way everyone else perceives us is a reflection of how we perceive ourselves.

Trippy, huh?

If you wake up one lucky morning thinking that you are the best thing walking the planet, you will make choices all day that reflect and further that belief. You'll put on the fancy perfume and wear your favorite jacket. You'll smile at the thoughtful guy who holds the door open for you at work and you'll speak to the nice lady behind the counter at the grocery store with extra confidence and certainty.

In the case of self-image, faking it till you make it is a pretty solid approach. If I'm going out with some friends, I'd much rather dress/walk/speak like I'm a total badass than behave like I think I'm boring and stupid. Wouldn't you? You can do this every day. You can wake up and decide, "Today, I think I want to be fascinating," and live your whole day from that place. You will go to bed later that night and find that you have indeed added more fascination to your life than usual. You do this for a couple of days solid and it starts becoming ingrained into your way of thinking and being, and then all of a sudden you don't have to work as hard at it. It starts to feel more and more authentic. It starts to feel like *you*.

The thing is that the rest of us don't know the difference. We don't know if you feel like the master of your own life or like an imposter. However, if you act like you've got it going on, we will believe you, and you will slowly start teaching us how to treat you. Then it all becomes beautifully cyclical; we will start treating you like a badass and you will actually begin feeling like one.

This happens to me onstage regularly. Sometimes before the show, I'll be feeling especially tired, worn down, and quite honestly more in the mood for a book and a bubble bath than a rock show. No matter. I do my hair and put on my stage clothes and warm up my voice anyway. Sometimes I'll even slip on some sexier-than-usual shoes to help give me a boost. I walk out on stage like I own it. Like this city built this stage especially for me. I look out at the crowd and try to stare right into their souls. I bring the mic to my lips and start singing my heart out as the voices of hundreds of people begin to drown out my own. It doesn't take thirty seconds before I have myself and the whole room convinced that I'm the queen of fucking England.

A few moments of faking it can equal a lifetime of making it.

Is the way you feel important or relevant to you?

_____

_____

_____

_____

_____

_____

How do you perceive yourself?

_____

_____

_____

_____

_____

_____

Is this different from how you wish you perceived yourself? If so, in what way?

_____

_____

_____

_____

_____

_____

_____

_____

_____

_____

_____

_____

_____

CHAPTER 12

ENJOYING THE WORK OF ART THAT IS YOU

I recently met this amazingly beautiful woman. She was backstage at one of our shows, and she looked like a freaking Barbie doll. I mean it. She was 5' 9" plus four inches of heels, and she had long blonde hair and perfect makeup. I'd never seen anything like her in real life.

I judged her immediately.

I figured she was one of the tour whores the other band kept bringing backstage after the shows, and I began mentally ripping her apart in seconds. This is something girls like to do to other girls when they are feeling insecure. There's no faster way to know you've got self-worth issues than if you meet someone and start making a mental list of all the reasons why they're below you.

I thought I was way past tearing other people down to feel good about myself, but it turns out I still have a long way to go. I mean, she was just *trying really hard, guys.* She was gorgeous, so I assumed she had nothing going for her but those classically good looks *(God, how boring!)* I briefly introduced myself to her, just to appear to be nice, and my thirty-second interaction with her convinced me that she was as stuck-up as she looked and that she thought she was better than me. *She's too pretty to be real. I bet her hair is all extensions and her lips are Botoxed. I bet her head is full of cotton candy.*

You can imagine what a fool I felt like when I had the chance to talk to her a few nights later and she was actually pretty awesome. Whoops. Turns out she was the girlfriend of several years of one of the band members, and she had a killer personality to back up her good looks. She was ambitious, funny, smart, and I felt totally inspired after talking with her. We exchanged numbers and plotted out the next time we'd get to tour together.

I had judged her for trying too hard, but after getting to know her, it actually kind of made me want to step up my game. I was in the middle of a rough and dirty tour and not feeling particularly great about myself, so her feminine energy was inspiring. I think that's why I was so quick to put her down—I felt threatened by this girl because she was rocking at something I was currently slacking in.

Over the next few days, I thought about how wrong I'd been to judge someone based on their looks, and I brainstormed how I could bring more beauty and femininity into my life while on the road. I committed to amping up some of the sexiness in my everyday life.

I wish that, as human beings, we could all be varying degrees and different types of fabulous and just let that be okay. I don't like walking by a beautiful woman and automatically analyzing whether she's prettier than me and why. I want the freedom to be my own kind of beautiful, and to not fear that the other people in the room are putting me down for it. I have experienced the wonder that comes from just letting everyone around me be their own kind of gorgeous. When this happens, there's no threat displays, no comparisons, no judgment—just that intoxicating, glorious freedom of us all being *ourselves.*

Judging and categorizing people within seconds of meeting them doesn't help anyone, least of all ourselves. I do myself no favors by stereotyping girls in bikinis with Barbie bodies as sluts or women who don't wear makeup as frumpy. There is room for all of us, and no one's appearance is better or worse than anyone else's. You'll find that the ease and grace that you begin to extend to other people when you internalize this will extend to the way you speak to yourself. By creating space for all different kinds of looks and just letting everyone do their thing without really thinking too much about it, it starts making space for you to show up in your own life without self-judgment. This is a beautiful thing.

~~~

In my personal self-love journey, I've been surprised and a little horrified to discover how much my personal body image keeps surfacing.

While I technically know that feeling beautiful and loving myself is totally *an inside job*, the honest truth is that my body and my face and my looks just won't stay out of it long enough for me to learn how to love myself 100% of the time. I've grown convinced that I can't separate self-love from how I feel about my body and my beliefs about my own beauty. It matters.

I am not a fan of this news, because that kinda means we have to be "beautiful" in order to love ourselves. Which—well, shit—disqualifies a lot of us, doesn't it? Especially if we're going by modern/Western standards of beauty.

When I get caught up in this way of thinking, it helps to imagine what life was like before modern art came around. Way back in the day, art only counted as art if it hit certain standards and had clean lines and actually looked like the scene or person that the artist was trying to recreate. Then Picasso and a bunch of other rebels came along and painted a bunch of crazy awesome stuff that started changing everyone's definition of art. All of a sudden, a term like "art" didn't just mean perfect technique or a dead-on resemblance to the rich noblewoman who'd commissioned the painting—it just meant an awesome combination of colors and textures and shapes that made people *feel* a certain way. Nowadays, art is a much broader concept, and we tend to celebrate a wide, creative range of what "beautiful art" means.

Lucky for us, "art" as a term has expanded. Sadly, "beauty" hasn't (Yet. It will.) Right now, beauty is as strict and boring a definition as art used to be before the rebels came on the scene and messed with it. Right now, women are only considered beautiful if we live up to certain standards—ones that we did not choose and have limited control over. Women (I say "women" here because women are disproportionately affected by society's "standards" of beauty, even though this phenomenon also deeply affects men) are breathtaking and multifaceted and colorful, but society won't slap the term "beautiful" on us if we don't fit its very narrow boundaries for the word. Let's expand the boundaries.

~~~

Growing up, I was first informed I was beautiful by my dad, who told me and my sister all the time. While I was grateful for this, even as a little kid I knew that dads kinda have to say this (the good dads, anyway), and after hearing it a hundred times, it didn't mean as much anymore.

When I was about 11, Mercedes had a passionate conversation with me about my looks. She sat me down. She proceeded to tell me I was *really hot*, and I was pleased with this good news. She had never steered me wrong before, so if she said I was a total hottie, I was in no position to question her. I'm so grateful for her decisive opinion on the issue and for the time she took to share it with me. I've drawn a lot of strength from conversations like that—ones where she's looked me in the eye and told me I can do, have, *be* anything—and she has, without question, shaped much of my self-image today because of this. Mercedes knows everything; if she said I was pretty back when I was 11, then that was that.

Isn't it strange how most of the time we have no real reference point for our own beauty, and pretty much find out if we are beautiful based on other people's critiques of us? If our parents told us from a young age we were worthless and ugly or kids at school picked on us because of our looks, then we get the message: we aren't beautiful, and this is a painful discovery. If we are sexually abused by our uncle who tells us how pretty and mature we are or the teenage boys at school send graphic texts to us detailing what they'd like to do to us, we get a different message—we are beautiful, but often this is not a welcome revelation.

I consider myself ridiculously fortunate that I first heard I was beautiful in the safety of my home and through something as harmless as a few talks with my big sister. I know that's usually not how it works, but I'm immensely grateful that it's how it happened for me.

~~~

Pop culture tells females from a young age that our value is defined by our sex appeal, and we are quick to play along. We dance in bikinis in rap videos to get exposure and maybe land a real acting job one day. We undo the top button of our blouse at work to get the promotion we seriously need. We run our fingers through our hair and bat our lashes to get out of speeding tickets. We know how to work our magic.

But all this magic-working is costing us something. Men need to stop viewing half of the world's population as just objects to have sex with, and as women, we need to stop using our bodies as bait to get what we want. Shine bright, show off what your mama gave you, but remember how much more you have to offer the world, too. You are good enough just because you're you; you deserve endless affection and respect, whether you choose to dress like Nicki Minaj or a Catholic nun.

My years being in such close proximity to men have totally informed my opinions on this. The touring world is undeniably male-dominated, and I've been privy to seeing how lots of guys' minds work up close and personal. What I've seen has disappointed and encouraged me all at once. There are plenty of unenlightened dudes out there perpetuating the broken system, dissecting women into nothing but body parts and generally being disrespectful, selfish assholes. Thankfully, there are also a lot of wonderful guys out there who repeatedly turn down the eager fangirl running up with a sharpie asking him to sign her boobs, offering a smile and a selfie instead.

Dudes get the same messages as women do about sex appeal, power, and self-image—just flipped and distorted through the same mirror. We are all playing by unfair rules, showing off touched-up photos of ourselves in exchange for likes and retweets. The standards that society feeds us shoot girls and guys in the feet equally, making guys think that every girl out there must look like a supermodel and girls think that they have to live up to that standard in order to even show their faces outside.

I imagine that if more of the Super Beautiful Models in magazines and on TV showed us what they really look like, we would all let out a sigh of relief. "Oh, thank God," we would exclaim under our breath, "Her skin isn't naturally flawless. Those cheekbones were drawn on in Photoshop. She has a little belly going on. She…looks kind of normal." Maybe then it'd be okay that we look kind of normal, too. Maybe then we could be okay with our A cups and bushy eyebrows and rounder tummies.

When I was 18, I gave up trying to keep up. I decided that wearing makeup was oppressive to women and that I wasn't going to give in to consumerism's lies telling me I had to have their products to be beautiful. I was good enough without all that extra primping stuff, and I was going to fight the system and show the world! Look how edgy and rebellious I am! I could be conventionally pretty if I tried, but I'm *not gonna try, so there!*

I remember sitting with Blake and Tyson, telling them yet again how stupid makeup was, and Tyson kindly pointing out to me that we'd had this talk before. "You know, Amy, it seems like this is really important to you. You bring it up a lot." It's like I wanted everyone to know that if I wasn't as pretty as my peers, it's only because they were cheating with their under-eye concealers and lip liners. We were playing by different rules.

Not wearing makeup is not for the faint of heart. You have to be a very special type of girl to live completely unfazed by the beauty standard, and to decide you love yourself just the way you are and that you want others to see and love you that way, too.

As it turns out, I am not that kind of girl. I usually feel self-conscious without makeup; I do not like passing by a mirror and feeling un-put-together. But I don't wear makeup for somebody else—I wear it for me, and I let myself enjoy it.

And guys? They say they like girls who don't wear makeup, but I think what they mean is they want a girl who looks "naturally beautiful"—usually with the help of makeup. Most boys don't know what girls actually look like because they only ever see us with our smoky eyes and rosy cheeks. Boys want our foundation to blend seamlessly in with our skin and our lip color to stay on when we kiss them. They want us to look beautiful, but they don't necessarily want to know how much makeup is actually involved in that process. I think that's what they mean when they say they don't like makeup.

More than anything, I feel misrepresented without makeup. I feel like the art project that I do on my face helps me portray a more accurate version of who I actually am on the inside. I can't say if that's liberating or really messed up, but I don't care either way. I've made peace with it, I enjoy it, and it's not going anywhere.

~~~

I love feeling beautiful—as in love, love, love it. It's one of my all-time favorite feelings. When I feel beautiful, I feel limitless. Watch out, world, because I cannot be stopped. The thing is, I don't even need to *look* beautiful to be limitless; I just have to *feel* like I am. For me, beauty is a feeling. Admittedly, a lot of times I need to check with the mirror to confirm whether or not I have "permission" to feel beautiful in that moment, but this is something I'm working on. Ideally, I would just feel gorgeous and radiant all the time.

But in the meantime, I've got a number of ways to get myself feeling beautiful. I meditate (okay, that's a loose term. It's more like, "I think nice things about myself."), I smile at myself in the mirror, and I celebrate natural beauty in others to help me love my own natural beauty. I also do more shallow, surface-y things like buy BB creams, watch YouTube beauty tutorials, and spend a healthy amount of time getting ready each morning, all in the hopes of achieving this feeling of beauty.

I don't know how else to say this, so I'll just put it out there: These things usually work. This is just like how we first approached self-love by setting up little external reminders and then began examining our beliefs. Usually, the more effort I put into my looks, the more beautiful I think I look, and, consequently, the more beautiful I feel.

If you're thinking, "um, duh," you must be a lot smarter than I am, because I had always assumed that feeling beautiful was an inside job and that no amount of perfectly applied eyeliner could fix insecurity. Turns out that's only half-true, and the eyeliner can be a valuable asset on the confidence journey.

The most important piece to this is figuring out where you stand and what you personally are comfortable with. I put effort into my looks for me, not for other people. I do it because it makes me feel good, and feeling good is awesome. Even if my motives are cloudy—even if I am maybe playing a game I don't believe in or perpetuating a deceitful beauty standard—that's not the point. I'm not committed to starting a makeup-free revolution; I just want to make peace with and enjoy the way I look. Find what works for you, and do it because you love it. Wear makeup or don't, dye your hair or don't, get tattoos or don't, but do it all with a clear conscience and without judgment of the people who do it differently from you. I think we can all help slow down the game by learning to have a little more compassion for ourselves and each other.

~~~

Most of us have been told at some point that we're flawed and don't make the cut. That hurts. Or maybe we've found out that we do make the cut, but often in a nasty, degrading way. That hurts, too.

But here's the thing: people telling you something about yourself *does not make it true.* If someone has told you that you are not beautiful, they lied. Pure and simple—they are wrong.

Try letting that thought bounce around in your head for a minute. Just consider it, even if it feels like a stretch for your brain.

If someone told you that you are one of the lucky ones who made the beauty cut, it doesn't really matter, does it? It mattered to me when my dad and sister told me I was beautiful, but only because I chose to take that and run with it. If you don't believe that you're beautiful, then people telling you so won't help you believe it, because you'll think they're just giving you empty compliments. It won't get through to you.

This is why it is so empowering to decide for yourself how beautiful you really are. To answer this question, once and for all:

"Am I beautiful?"

There is so much peace waiting for you on the other side when you're able to authentically answer that question with a whole-hearted *yes*. It's a holistic yes that says "Uh-huh, I belong here. Yes, I deserve love. Yes, I am a work of art."

When you make up your own mind on that, you don't live or die by other people's assessments of you. You know that when people compliment or critique you, they are simply telling you where they think you fall on *the cultural measuring line of what is currently considered beautiful.*

You can work your butt off to measure up—and a lot of us do just that—but you will never be good enough. If you're trying to come out on up of whatever magazines and TV personalities and models and movie stars and fashion designers call "beautiful," you will never, ever be beautiful enough; that standard is constantly evolving new and improved ways to make us normal people feel inadequate. And even if you are a focused, determined student, even if you set your mind to figure it out and become so gorgeous that the world bows at your feet—it won't actually help. If I hated myself before I was beautiful, I'll still hate myself after. You don't feel more beautiful by moving up on the beauty ladder; you get that feeling by learning to love yourself.

So let's stop using that twisted beauty scale as an accurate measurement of our own value. Stop ranking yourself and other people. Begin to train your mind to see beauty differently, both in yourself and in others. Now, when a Victoria's Secret model comes on the screen I challenge myself not to think, "Oh my God, she's so pretty, I wish I were her!" but to think instead, "Western society is currently digging big boobs and tan skin and pouty lips, and she's rocking that look." Cool, but kind of irrelevant on my own beauty journey.

Some wonderful things happen when we stop ranking everybody on the made-up Shallow Beauty Scale and stop using the moving target of what a handful of people are telling us is hot this year as our personal beauty gospel. We start viewing individuals as whole people rather than a composite of their facial features and body parts. The plain, stringy-haired checkout lady who has "let herself go" is actually a fascinating work of human art standing right in front of you, with dreams and opinions and, hey, you have the chance to positively influence her day instead of judging her! You can impact her world by smiling at her and acknowledging her—instead of raising your eyebrows at her looks in order to appease the mean little voice in your head that's trying to make you feel better about yourself by putting her down.

This translates to everyone around you, and it's infectious. You get to enjoy beauty everywhere you go. You begin seeing unique traits as fascinating and beautiful to look at. Bold noses, button noses, thin lips, fat lips, defined jaws and round faces: you can begin to see the beauty in all of it. This helps untrain your mind that there is just one standard beauty mold, and it helps you to enjoy a host of features, skin tones, and body types you would have otherwise scoffed at as somehow not meeting the bar.

Once you start letting yourself truly appreciate humanity in all its different shapes and sizes, you can stop judging yourself by the ridiculous standards you've been holding yourself to, as well. You can look in the mirror and be excited by your own unique nose, your own shapely frame. A whole world of beauty opens up to us when we stop using society's dominant views on beauty as our standard of measurement. We're all works of art.

~~~

If viewing pretty much everything and everyone as beautiful feels too much for you at first, try being the beauty standard instead. That means exactly what it sounds like it means: You decide that you are the ideal.

Crazy, right? *You are the beauty standard. You are what you're supposed to look like.*

A great place to begin is singling out neutral body parts and facial characteristics—things about yourself you don't care either way about—and imagine that they're actually the best thing ever. Start with something you don't feel too strongly about, like maybe your fingers. Study them. Imprint their shapes and features in your mind, and then make up your mind that these are the most perfect fingers in the world. They are just the right length and shape, and your skin looks exactly how it should. That's settled, then. Your fingers are making the beauty cut. Your fingers are beautiful. You don't have to worry about those anymore.

Taking a neutral body part and framing it as a positive—even freaking awesome—is how you train your mind to rewrite the beauty standard in your favor.

Your cheeks, lips, eyes, nose, skin color, boobs, legs, tummy? They all make the cut! In fact, they *define* the cut.

When you spend some time thinking this way about yourself on purpose, you find yourself accepting and actually appreciating so many of your unique and beautiful features. I have totally changed the way I see myself when I look in the mirror now. I am emotionally attached to my own face and body. I'm committed. I'm in. I've decided that I look exactly the way I was created to look, and I let myself love my own beautiful self. I totally still have bad days when all of that goes out the window and I fall back into the pit of judging myself against others, but I know now that I can—and should—always come back to my own standards of beauty, because they're the ones that actually matter.

~~~

Here's what I know for sure: I have way bigger things to do with my life than obsess over how I am or am not meeting another person's stupid, made-up ideals for how I look. You do, too. We have bigger shit to do, to *be*. We create our own freedom by not hyperfocusing on and correcting "flaws." I have big things to accomplish in my lifetime, and I plan to let my beauty serve my heart instead of spending my precious heart energy worrying about damaged hair or imperfect skin.

Remember that you are a walking, talking, breathing work of art, and just because the rest of the world doesn't always recognize your beauty doesn't mean you're not worthy of love, or respect, or attention. We are undiscovered treasures, works of precious art hidden in plain sight. Let's not wait for someone to come along and discover us and validate what we've suspected all along: that we are fucking masterpieces. Let's live a life of courageous expression, continually revealing our various textures and nuances and radiating our beauty out into the world.

Need some suggestions on how to amp up that shine? Check it out:

- Realize you're straight-up delusional about how much people notice your "flaws" that you can't stop obsessing over. Nobody of consequence worries about them.

- Don't feed into this perfection thing—don't hyper-edit your social media shots, and don't zoom in on a picture on your phone or your face in the mirror to pick away at the features you hate. Don't magnify their importance in your life.

- Get some perspective. Are you pretty healthy? Does your body do the things that you need it to do to carry you through this life, even if it's not perfect? These are really, really big wins.

- Don't labor under the delusion that super-gorgeous people are necessarily any happier than you. If they haven't done the inside work that you're doing right now, then they'll unfortunately probably rip themselves apart, too. You have as much a shot at this self-love thing as anybody else.

- Practice checking yourself out with love. Play around and find what parts of yourself you *do* like. Focus on that feeling so that it can expand to other parts of yourself. Never leave a mirror holding a negative opinion of yourself. If you catch yourself thinking, "God, I look awful," stop and challenge yourself to think something else. Find something positive like, "I like how I look in these jeans." Make it a habit to end your interactions with yourself on a good note.

Do you regularly feel beautiful? If yes, describe when/why. If no, write down what you imagine it must feel like to feel beautiful every day:

_____

_____

_____

_____

_____

_____

_____

What are some things that you can do or think to help you feel more beautiful, more of the time?

_____

_____

_____

_____

_____

_____

How would you like to start working these things into your everyday life?

_____

_____

_____

_____

_____

_____

CHAPTER 13

TAKING BACK YOUR POWER WITH INTENTIONALITY

There's this thing I do when I sing called "audiating" that I learned from Melissa Cross's *The Zen of Screaming*. Normal, everyday singing is pretty casual—you just kind of do it. Most people sing on autopilot without really having to think about it. You sing the pitch you know is next and it usually sounds okay.

Audiating is just like singing, but on *purpose*. It is the mental practice of hearing the note in your head before you actually sing it, and this makes all the difference in the world. When your brother sings happy birthday at your party he probably doesn't have to try too hard, but when you're singing for a living, it's something worth putting the effort into. When you audiate, you take care to mentally pause before a certain note and hear that note in your head before you sing it. You take a millisecond to think about it and aim for it, and this greatly improves your accuracy. It isn't realistic to do for every note, because you can't give all the notes that kind of attention, but it is perfect for those money notes where you want to impress everyone with how awesome you sound.

This is also how I'm learning to live my life on purpose.

Just like singing, I could just jump in and do it, or I can add another layer of thoughtfulness and take a moment to think about it beforehand. I can pause to make sure I nail it. Also just like singing, it would be impractical for every little thing, like buttering your toast, but it's perfect for important moments, like a first date or a job interview, and it gets more natural with practice.

This may sound harsh, but I believe it with all my heart: If you aren't living intentionally, you're straight-up doing it wrong. I did life wrong for years. I thought I had no control over what happened to me and over my level of happiness. I thought that life just sort of unfolded around me, and that it was my job to react to whatever came my way. I know better now.

Now, I know that loving ourselves means crafting a life we love, too. It means believing that we really, *really* deserve joy, and it means going after that joy with a steady, intentional focus. Most of us live our lives rather passively, humming along, letting life happen to us. That way sucks—now I have every intention of happening to my life. I want to feel confident that where I'm going is where I want to end up.

A lot of smart, well-meaning, New-Age-y people bring up the wisdom of things like *trusting the process* and *waiting to see what the universe will do.* That's nice and all, but it doesn't work for me. The control freak in me just doesn't do well when told to "wait and see." Almost nothing good in my life has come from waiting around for things to happen. Usually, I'm glad that I said something. Nine times out of ten, stepping in was the right move. This has taught me to be more active in my decisions and in my dreams.

For the most part, good things happen in my life because I very intentionally go after them. That's how I healed from self-hatred, that's how I'm learning to love myself, and that's how I've gotten a lot of the awesome opportunities in my life and career. The more energy I put towards something, the better the results. The flavor of the energy I bring to these things matters, too. I don't want to be desperate; I want to feel clearheaded and deserving while I go after what I desire. We're going for "intentionality" here, not necessarily "intensity."

Believe me—I know all about staying up late at night, plotting endless scenarios of how I can get what I want out of life. I know what it's like to see someone else living *my* dream, and feeling all the anxiety and want that comes along with that. I know how to want something vividly, desperately, intensely.

It's a real pain in the ass.

Wanting something so severely like that uses up a lot of precious energy—energy that I could be putting towards actually *taking* the steps that need to be taken for my dream to materialize.

You can do it, be it, have it—whatever that "it" is for you. Whatever you want for your life, whatever you find yourself craving, desiring, and dreaming of can be yours.

The only thing that separates you from the people who already are where you want to be is that they went and got it. That's it! It's yours, my friend. It's got your name written all over it.

So what's stopping you?

You probably have a number of compelling answers to that question. You likely have a dozen convincing reasons why. I know I did. Stuff like:

"I'm not ready yet."

"I don't have the money/support/talent."

"It's out of my control."

"I'm not qualified."

"I don't deserve it."

That last one there—I don't deserve it—that's a big one. That belief lurks deep down in the bottom of most of our hearts and minds. When a thought like that is hidden in the dark, the best way I've found to deal with it is to expose it by dragging it out into the light.

"I don't deserve it" is a belief that takes over everything. It shows up as self-sabotage in major ways and in smaller, subtler ways. If you think you don't deserve love, then you won't look her in the eye when she's talking to you. If you think you don't deserve human kindness, then you won't say thank you when he holds the elevator door for you. If you believe you don't deserve happiness, then you will keep finding a way back to your sadness.

If you think you don't deserve your dream, you'll certainly fail.

From where I stand, you deserve it. We all do. The joy, the peace, the love, the dream—all of it. But that issue of worthiness can keep you from having any of it.

~~~

So here's what you do: Spend some time to focus on this. Put your energies towards exposing this mindset—this lie—and replacing it with the truth. Pay attention to your thoughts, because otherwise they will come and go in your mind without you even questioning them. Use your new thought-babysitting skills to rewrite the lie of unworthiness.

Tell yourself in advance to be on the lookout for the "I don't deserve this" thoughts. Put them on your radar. This way, when you find yourself thinking, "Oh, hey, I just saw that happy looking person and thought to myself, *I could never be that happy*," you're free to identify it for the imposter that it is and go on to think something positive and true on *purpose*. Something like, *Actually, I can have as much happiness in my life as I want. There is an unlimited quantity of joy with my name on it, and I refuse to believe that I'm somehow disqualified from this. It's my motherfreaking birthright.*

You deserve a really wonderful, fulfilling, badass life. Not in a weird, entitled sort of way, where you believe that just because you're you, life should bring everything you want to your doorstep. It doesn't work like that. But the thing is, I'm guessing that most of us don't have that problem—we have the opposite problem, in which we fear that we probably deserve a really miserable life. It doesn't have to be that way, and that's what I hope you'll begin believing—that you really can have happiness, and success, and self-love. It's yours.

I like to view life like a big buffet table on a cruise ship or at a fancy hotel. The table is set up in the middle of the room, and piled on top is everything we could ever want out of life. Your dream career, happiness, personal fulfillment, out-of-this-world relationships—they're all on there for the taking.

However, most of humanity is gathered along the outskirts of the room, hugging the walls, scanning all the wonderful offerings on the table but too scared and insecure to actually go get anything.

"Do you see that dream over there? I would *really* like to have that."

"Oh, wow, look at that self-love, that looks amazing. Who is in charge here? Who do I see about getting on the waiting list for that?"

We're all sheepishly eyeing the table, timidly throwing out hopes and wishes and metaphorically starving to death while everything that nourishes us sits ten feet away on the table, waiting for us to snatch it up.

Then there are some people who literally just walk up and get what they need. They just grab it. Those of us waiting around eyeing the table think to ourselves, "Wait, what? Can she do that? Can she just walk in and grab hope? I've been craving that thing for years!" It's enough to jolt some of us awake and give us the courage to also walk up and take what we need.

That's how a lot of life works. If you want something, go get it. Not in a selfish, greedy way, but in a way that honors your needs and respects your desires. You going and getting what you want does not leave the rest of the world empty-handed. There is enough love to go around—we can all have a giant piece of that. And what's so powerful is that, by you going and getting what you want, it inspires the rest of us to do the same. We see you and we think, "Oh, she just went and got it? I could probably do that, too." It's a very powerful, generous way to live.

This works with all kinds of things. Not getting enough respect from your boss or your partner? Go grab *respect* off the buffet table by cultivating an undeniable sense of self-respect no one can ignore. Not happy with your job? Grab *initiative* off the table and check out an online course to expand your skills or start your own business on the side. Feeling unqualified to live your dream? Take *permission* off the table and allow it to soak into your heart.

Rest is another thing available for the taking, and this has been a pretty personal one for me. After years of being in this industry, I'm finally learning that no one will carve out a chance to rest for me. No one will tell me to take a day off or give me permission to sleep in. I have to create my own rest.

We were on an especially grueling tour awhile back, and my limits were being pushed to the max. Each day was filled with intense load-ins, multiple meet-and-greets, vocal work, and long hours at the merch table, plus a show to play and a daily class to teach. About a month in, I was feeling really exhausted. Actually, I was feeling worn out about a week in, but I just kept pushing myself for several more weeks because I didn't want to come off as lazy or uncommitted.

One day, I finally realized I could chill out if I wanted to. I could carve a few things off the schedule. I didn't *have* to do three meet-and-greets a day or sell merch for hours on end. I could grab *rest* off the buffet table and put my name on it; and since no one was gonna do it for me, I just did it for myself. I told the band I needed to back off for a little bit, and nobody seemed to mind. If anything, they were surprisingly supportive. It was scary to do—sitting in the bus sipping coffee while my bandmates swarmed around me, working like normal. I had to fight the guilt and the thoughts that my team secretly resented me for drawing some boundaries, but once I created some rest for myself, I was able to see the insanity of our workload. Yes, a lot needed to be done, but for the most part, we just all really *like to work*. We had become somewhat addicted to the buzz of feeling busy and productive. We had gotten on the let's-work-really-hard-for-our-dream train and had never stepped off. But I was *tired*—we all were tired—and I figured it was time I made space for rest.

So what are you craving? What is missing from your life? Remember, it will not jump off the table and land in your lap. Go get what you need.

The perfect place to add more intentionality to our lives is in our mornings. Mornings are their own kind of special; they're maybe the most precious time of day. They are fresh, fragile, delicate little things, promising us the loveliest of days if only we can manage to start them off right. I've always been partial to those early hours of the day, but road life is not kind to early risers, making a total mockery of any morning rituals I might want to engage in. On tour, I've learned to settle for five hours of sleep and maybe thirty seconds of mindfulness while brushing my teeth followed by a desperate attempt to recite gratitude lists in the back of the van while six guys jacked up on Starbucks act like zoo animals all around me. It's a joke.

This is why I like to take special care to make my mornings at home as big of a deal as possible. When I first wake up, I spend several minutes getting into the right frame of mind, and I've developed some pretty awesome morning practices. When we're off-tour, I sleep in until a solid 8:30 a.m. When I'm up, I go into my sewing/piano room, and on ideal, spacious days, I don't come out until 10:30. Take that, tour schedule.

On the best of mornings, the good stuff will start even before I get out of bed. Sometimes, when I remember, I will wake up intentionally thinking something wonderful. I will let myself feel grateful, and I will physically smile. I'll think as many good things as I can. This is all "on purpose," intentional stuff to combat the natural, autopilot thoughts that always hit me, like the workload ahead of me, the stupid things I did or said yesterday, and everything else in my life that's not working.

It is so helpful to take advantage of the space that comes with early mornings—I find that my heart is softer and more open to change then than at any other time of the day. If I can get myself going in the right direction first thing in the morning, my whole day can be magical.

I've listed out some of my favorite ways to start my day here so that you can see if any would be right for you. I rarely do all of these, but even just picking one that inspires you can be mega-helpful.

When all else fails, try caffeinating. Seriously. God speaks through coffee, and we all know it.

OUTSIDE CONTENT

A lot of mornings, I am too tired and lazy to think all these wonderful things first thing, so I drag myself out of bed and watch something brilliant online. I can't always bring my heart to that happy, content place on my own, so I have to call in the big guns, a.k.a. motivational speakers on YouTube. There is so much awesome, inspiring content online, and I have my favorite go-to's that I turn on when I need a little extra help. It's pretty much like a healthy brainwashing session to get me in the right headspace. There have been many mornings where I will pause the video with tears in my eyes, in awe of the relevancy of the topic that day. Some of my faves include inspiring TED Talks, interviews with my favorite authors, and every once in a while, I'll mix in good ol' Tony Robbins. Hate all you want, guys, but that dude is like an espresso shot of pure positivity.

GRATITUDE

When I've woken up a little more, I sometimes do this awesome gratitude thing where I bring to mind (and often write down) everything that is right in my life. It's like taking stock of my life, but only focusing on the good stuff. Things like, "Oh my gosh, I am 100% healthy and nobody close to me is dying and there is heat in my home and leftover Chinese in my fridge. I have it crazy good." See if you can surprise yourself with how detailed you can be, because otherwise you tend to get bored being thankful for the same, big things every day, and it loses the effect. At least, that's what always happens to me.

For a long time, I thought the point of gratitude lists was just, well, to be thankful and stuff. To make an effort to list out all the things I am grateful for. But I've been learning that the point is more like *cultivating a sense of wellbeing*. Instead of throwing my thank-yous up at the sky, pacifying heaven so it keeps sending good things my way, it's actually much more fun to sit with the feeling of "Here is everything that is good and right in my life." This is so much better. It transforms the process from a feeling of duty (thank you for my mama and breakfast and sunshine and music and…) to a look into all the amazing things in your life that are currently working out. Often, there are more than you think there are if you just take a moment or two to list them out and sit with them for a bit. Our thank-yous have the capacity to nurture the world and ourselves, and there is so much to be gained when we sit with our wellbeing.

JOURNALING THE DAY AHEAD

One of my favorite daily practices goes like this: I think of the day ahead and write down everything that is going to completely suck. I have those thoughts lurking in the back of my head anyway, and I find that getting them out of my head and onto paper is so incredibly helpful to me. I write down things like, "Our band meeting will drag on forever and when I try to bring up the set list changes the guys won't let me change any of it and our show will suck because of it," or, "I haven't done laundry in a week and I have nothing I'd like to wear today," or, "I have to do that conference call and I know I haven't prepped for it like I should have and it's gonna be awkward and suck." This process helps me recognize subconscious areas of tension and fear in my day.

When I write things down, I often realize how ridiculous a lot of these things sound, especially in light of all I have to be grateful for. Because of this, I always, without exception, follow this list up with its counterpart: every reason why today is going to be freaking amazing! This list is always longer, and way more fun to write. Stuff like, "It's going to be sunny today and the snow is gonna melt! (I add obnoxious exclamation points to the end of these phrases to really drive the point home). My sister is coming over and we're gonna drink tea and talk about nothing! I can't wait to work on the new song I started last night! The band is buying lunch today!"

What has been especially awesome about this is that, a lot of the time, I find myself taking neutral daily events and rewriting them as ultra-positive things. Events that could fall into either category (I have to go grocery shopping today) can turn into "I am so excited to go to the store; I am going to listen to my favorite playlist on the way there, and I can't wait to get all this amazing produce to make smoothies with, and I am most definitely getting chocolate chips so I can bake tonight."

Try it. It sounds simple—even silly—but it can change everything for the better.

VISUALIZE THE DAY

After I've written my bad/good list detailing the day, I'm in a perfect position to visualize it. "Visualize" is the grown-up word for "use your imagination." I close my eyes and briefly imagine myself in situations that I know I will find myself in that day. In each situation, I pause and picture how I'm interacting (kindly, gently), and how I'm feeling (vibrant, present) in that moment.

As an example, let's say I am playing a big show that night and I know I'll be met with some anxiety in the hours leading up to our performance. Instead of worrying about the impending anxiety, I picture myself at the venue, calm and full of joy to be there. I picture myself side stage, about to go on, bursting with confidence and light ready to be shared. I see myself on stage, pleasantly surprising myself with how good I feel, and lastly, I picture myself after the show, feeling accomplished and grateful. This creates a killer mental picture for my subconscious hard drive about what I want to have happen today—as far as I can control it.

It really helps to take a moment to pause and picture an event or situation before it occurs (This is a great example of audiating in action.) I imagine the people I'll see, what I'll be wearing, and the things I'll probably talk about. I try to recognize tempting pitfalls to avoid—

stuff like feeling self-conscious around successful people or feeling frustrated with myself for dominating the conversation.

I can decide in advance how I want to feel, and let that influence how I will choose to behave. I always want to be friendly and considerate rather than stuck in my own head. I want to feel interesting and self-assured instead of boring or insecure. I really, really want to feel present in that moment instead of wishing I were somewhere else. I take a few minutes and picture myself experiencing all these good feelings, and this primes me to actually feel them when I get to wherever I'm going.

My moments of intentionality also help me identify potential self-inflicted tragedies that I might run into. I'm often unkind to myself in social settings, but I can help avoid that by being aware of my tendency to go down that road. I know that after an interaction with someone whose opinion I care about, I am especially hard on myself. I almost always feel like I talked too much and said something stupid after the fact. Knowing this in advance helps me make sure I don't go there and helps me be nicer to myself on the car ride home.

Try to start your mornings by spending a few moments picturing the day ahead. What are you most excited about, and how can you get as much joy out of that experience as possible? What are you dreading or worried about? Do you want to spend all day dreading that, or is there another approach you can take? And, most importantly, how can you be present all day long and feel happy in your own skin? Spending some time answering these questions each morning can change everything.

MINDFUL SATISFACTION

Lastly, when I go to bed at night, I like to intentionally allow myself to feel satisfied with the day. I have a habit of running a mental checklist of everything I didn't get done or that I screwed up on that day, and that's a horrible state of mind to be in while ending the day. I fight this by taking a few seconds to go over everything good that happened that day and everything I am grateful for, and then I feel satisfied with myself and my life, regardless of my circumstances.

I should note that, sometimes, a weird and twisted part of me resists all these awesome rituals I've made up. Something in me *does not want* to be thankful for or excited about the day ahead, and that same something doesn't want me to feel good about everything I've accomplished when I go to bed at night. I feel like I'm dealing with a strong-willed toddler, kicking and screaming until she exhausts herself and falls asleep in my arms.

I've learned that I can't let my resistance to joy freak me out, and that I can't read too much into it. *I can't overthink it.* When all else fails and I simply can't get my heart to cooperate, I show myself who's boss by starting the day anyway and acting as content as can be. It's a trick, and my stubborn heart falls for it every time. "Oh, everything's good after all? Okay."

Sometimes you have to gently take your heart by the hand to show it the way, just like you would for a child.

Where do undeserving beliefs show up in your life?

_____

_____

_____

_____

_____

_____

What do you need to grab off the buffet table?

_____

_____

_____

_____

_____

_____

What are some ways you could add more intentionality to your life?

_____

_____

_____

_____

_____

_____

_____

CHAPTER 14

JOY HUNTING

When we love ourselves, we take care to make sure that we're happy. Because it matters to us, we care what the person in the mirror has to say about our life. We listen, we collect little signs, and we take notes so we can do our very best at continually adding joy to our lives.

Happiness has not been especially easy for me. It has not fallen into my lap, and I am not a naturally blissful and carefree human being. Happiness has come to me with much patience and much intentionality. Sometimes I feel like I'm clawing my way towards it, but that usually doesn't make it any easier. I've had to learn the hard way what does.

I will say that I am grateful that I've gotten to take the long way to joy, because I know the path a lot better now than I would have if I'd simply bumped into happiness on accident or if it had been all I'd ever known. This puts me in a really good spot to be able to recreate my journey for myself and for others and to show people who also may not be naturally inclined towards happiness how in the world I got to this place.

Nothing stands between me and my joy. She is right here, as native as my soul, as close as my skin. Sometimes, she comes to me and gives me her presence as a gift—a gift for which I did nothing at all to earn. But much more often, I hear her when I listen for her. When I pause and acknowledge her. Come to think of it, this is the same way I often interact with God. God and joy may very well be made of the same stuff.

At the risk of stating the obvious, you can be as happy as you wanna be, for as many days in a row as you wanna be. I often fall into the trap of believing that if life is good for so many days in a row, then any day now I'm gonna inevitably wake up and have a bad day. It doesn't have to work like that. Your days can keep getting better and better, building joy upon joy as you learn how to feed your heart happy truths. Don't buy into the lie that there's only so much joy to go around. Joy self-multiplies, so be selfish and lean into joy. Take as much as you want.

When I'm feeling off, I've learned to ask myself: *How would I be-have/think/move if I were happy right now?* This is a really awesome question that disrupts negativity and creates instant possibilities. Just asking it is powerful, but following through and doing whatever I came up with is even better.

Here's another question—two, actually: Do you know what joy is? Have you felt it?

If yes, take a second and think about some of the times when you've felt real joy.

If not, try imagining what joy might feel like if it ever came your way. Where are you? Who is with you? How does it all feel in your body? Your mind? Your heart?

Joy resonates with every cell in our body because it is our original state, what we were created to feel and to live in. Joy is breathtaking and wonderful and one of my very favorite things. I actually think it's probably everybody's favorite thing; they just maybe haven't given it that name yet.

Joy is a lot like "happy," but better. Joy is *rich*. Joy is *deep*. Happy is like margarine; joy is like butter (you can taste the difference). It is authentic, the real deal, and it is your true nature. Joy is what you were created for. Joy is what you're searching for when you impulse buy, when you eat your feelings, when you lie around in bed all day watching reruns, when you get high, when you jump from partner to partner without finding what you're looking for.

It took me too long to learn where to find joy, but now that I know where she hides, I can find her everywhere.

I can see now that one of the reasons it took me so long was because its simplicity kept tripping me up. When I finally realized where joy lives, I was actually sort of disappointed. I genuinely thought that joy lived on the other side of achieving your goals and dreams for your life, which, if you're most of us, consists of being rich and famous. Turns out, joy doesn't live on the other side of anything. It lives here. In fact, if you can't feel joy where you are, you won't feel it when you get your life together and accomplish your dreams, either.

Joy, I have learned, lives in the simplest of things. In these tiny little moments hidden in a million places throughout the day. That's why I was a little taken aback; I wanted joy to be flashier, more glamorous. But the good news about its simplicity is its accessibility; anybody that wants to can have it, right now.

Joy lives in places that seem silly to the hardened soul. You have to have an open, soft heart to find her, and I think the softer your heart gets, the more easily you'll see her.

After I realized that joy lives in simple, easy things, I started keeping a list of places to find her so I wouldn't get confused again if I ever forgot. Nowadays, I keep a running list of things that bring joy, and I am always on the lookout for new things to add, as I keep discovering joy in more and more places.

I like to think of these things as Old People Things, because old people have this stuff figured out. When I was a kid, I didn't understand the value of any of this; I wanted to watch TV and eat Swiss Cake Rolls. But old people could sit on a porch and watch a pie cool and be happy. That's the stuff I'm talking about.

Here's a list of experiences where I'm pretty certain joy likes to hide:

Eating a ripe strawberry in the summer sunshine that you picked yourself.

Wrapping a baby in a blanket and smelling her forehead and kissing her cheeks.

Gathering around people you love at the winter holidays.

Enjoying an amazing homemade meal with your friends.

Making art from your soul and sharing it with others.

A September walk among fall leaves while wearing your favorite scarf.

Noticing and appreciating flowers as they start to bloom in spring.

Moving your body in a fresh new way at yoga.

Your favorite hot drink in a buzzing coffee shop in your favorite part of town.

Curling up with a novel on the porch while smelling the lilac blooms around you.

See what all this stuff has in common? It's all really simple, affordable stuff. It's actually kind of…normal. And if this list didn't exactly sweep you off your feet to go on a nature walk, I don't blame you. It's taken me a long time to connect to these easy, almost cliché things as actual pathways to joy. All I can say is this: Don't resist. Joy lives in the simple things, and we tend to brush past simple things all the time in our busy modern lives.

My most authentic and enjoyable moments of joy usually come from three places: people, nature, and food. Oh yeah, and one more:

art. Art is a real source of joy, too. So I guess a good word to sum up where joy comes from is "creation"—in every sense of the word.

Maybe you don't believe me. Maybe your experience is that joy actually lives in cool, big moments like getting a new job, or shopping sprees, or winning backstage passes to see your favorite band. And that's awesome—let yourself feel the excitement of those things. But I'd be hesitant to limit myself to thinking that joy primarily lives in that big, shiny stuff, because that's not everyday life for most of us. That adrenaline rush, that euphoric high of a new and exciting adventure—yeah, it's awesome, but not exactly the same as joy.

When I was a little kid, every once in a great while we'd get to go to Chuck-E-Cheese on a class trip. I *lived* for those days. Or my birthday? Highlight of the freaking year. And that's totally cool; I'm glad I had fun and exciting events in my young life, but there were a lot of other cool sources of joy in between those big events that I didn't even consider until later. Getting to play princess and cowboy with my brother Ben was nice and all, but I didn't really lean in and savor those moments; we were, after all, just passing the time until dinner. Getting to watch Noah as a baby was all right, but I didn't realize how much joy could be gained from those precious moments of playing with him or singing him to sleep until I was an adult. I only saw the pleasure in big things like summer camp, pizza parties, and Six Flags days. Everything else was just boring, normal life, waiting for another cool event to happen.

Now I know better, and it's made all the difference. There is joy to be found in all sorts of places throughout my day, and I serve myself well by honoring and recognizing them instead of diminishing them because they don't release buckets of endorphins all at once.

A good life is one that's full of precious, tiny moments, all day long. That still blows my mind. I am much more naturally inclined to think that a good life should mean getting ahead and being super successful at what you set out to do. If a good life is defined by enjoying simple moments, that means that the hippie drifter who crashes on friends' couches has just as good of a shot at joy as, say, Katy Perry.

Not fair, right? What's even more unfair is that that guy probably has even *more* of a chance at finding joy since his life is by definition simpler and slower than Katy's. She will probably have to work twice as hard to find moments of stillness and simplicity in which to feel joy as he will.

Start looking for these moments. Find your thing. Be on the look-out every day for small, simple moments of joy. Start keeping a list in your journal or on your phone of what makes you happy, even if it's not these little, simple things at first—you'll get the hang of it. Take the time to notice the pretty coffee art in your cappuccino mug and let your senses experience that first sip for all the wonder it contains. Open your blinds slowly, with intention, and soak in the sunlight for a second or two each morning. If it's raining, close your eyes and savor the sound of the drops. Don't write this stuff off! It is seriously these little moments of *noticing* that have made my life exponentially more joyful rather than the big successes and strides.

~~~

One more thing about joy.

I mentioned earlier that I thought maybe joy and God were made of the same stuff, and I really do think I'm onto something there. After years of my spirituality being a source of anxiety for me, to think of God as one with joy is huge.

If you have been raised ultra-religiously and you are starting to suspect that something's a little off—maybe you're miserable more than you are happy, or your relationship with God is more a source of panic than bliss—I suggest considering backing off a little. I've had a lot of success with exposing myself to other teachings and sources of hope besides Christianity, and this has put spirituality into perspective for me. It wasn't easy to do; researching doctrine that wasn't "Biblical" went against every bone in my body, and I often found myself feeling like I had to repent after reading about any spiritual perspective other than the one I grew up with.

Even though it was a challenge, it loosened me up a bit and gave me a fresh perspective on God—one that is so much better than the narrow one I'd carried of him before. I grew up viewing God as something like a Mary Kay consultant; kind, but mostly interested in enlisting as many people as possible, and once we were on the team, it was our job to sign more people up.

After intentionally putting my heart in front of more open-minded readings, I was pleased to find that a much more open, awesome view of God was within my reach if I wanted it. If you've been raised on one hardcore belief system, you can bring some balance to all that intensity by venturing out a bit and exposing yourself to other ways of thinking. If you grew up with beliefs similar to mine, you probably learned that you have the spirit of God living inside of you, and if you've placed your "salvation" in his hands, God is big and kind enough to stay close to you as you wander and explore. Everything in you might wrestle and scream that you are abandoning your faith just by reading about other ways of viewing the world, but this is actually giving you an amazing opportunity. By looking into all of your options, suddenly you have a chance to *choose* God and choose your beliefs—and this is a luxury that many of us raised in a church from birth never had.

I gravitate towards a lot of really awesome, freeing, New-Age ways of looking at the world. I know a lot of Christians automatically associate "New Age" with "demonic" (hi, Mom!), and believe me, my ultra-conditioned Christian brain tends to freak out in the midst of my explorations more often than not. In those moments, I calm down, ask God to guide my spiritual journey, and remember that I have "discernment" (Christians love that word). God has a vested interest in making sure I don't go off the spiritual deep end and come out with crazy, nonsensical beliefs on the other side. He can handle my travels, and I think he even encourages them.

Today, I feel a bit like a recovering ex-Christian, and I have happily traded in *Christianity* for *spirituality*. Sometimes I still worry that I'm doing spirituality wrong (shouldn't I be praying more? Is God pissed at me for not reading the Bible?) but I've got to say, the peace in my life speaks for itself. I've learned I can't follow preconditioned ideas of God, so instead I follow love, peace, wonder, and—yes—joy.

I have not found God through weeping and fervent prayer and strict obedience. I imagine he is just as bored with these things as I am. I *have* found him in the most wonderful of places: in joy. Every morning I rise and I find God yet again in the sunshine streaming in through the bus windows, in the people I love and—on the really great days—in the woman smiling back at me in the mirror. I have learned that God often does not hide in self-denial and sacrifice. He lives in the very center of joy, because he is joy.

Where do you find real, actual joy?

_____

_____

_____

_____

_____

_____

_____

_____

_____

_____

What are some ways that you could bring more small moments of joy into your everyday life?

_____

_____

_____

_____

_____

_____

Is your spirituality a source of joy for you?

_____

_____

_____

_____

_____

_____

CHAPTER 15

ACCEPTING YOURSELF AND YOUR LIFE

I've talked to thousands of fans over the last few years that unashamedly wanted the job I have. At every meet-and-greet, there's always somebody asking, "How did you get here?"

I've grown convinced that everybody kinda wants to be a rockstar.

I love that! I love seeing their passion and their fierce desire to be up on that stage, influencing the crowd. I love that fans see their heroes in music videos tearing it up and think *I want to do that*. I mean, if you're reading this book, you probably at one time in your life wanted to be a rockstar, right?

Cue the cynic: Well, you know, we can't all be rockstars. Someone has to be in the audience. Someone has to *listen* to all that music that the rest of us so desperately want to *make*.

The thing is, I think this ingrained desire to be a successful musician isn't exactly what it looks like. I'm pretty sure it has way more to do with the *idea* behind being a rockstar more than the actual practicals of the job description. I think everybody wants to be loved and admired. Everyone wants to make important work and have people resonate with it. Everyone wants the freedom to be the boldest version of themselves and have people adore them for it—and maybe even pay them for it. These are pretty awesome desires.

Clearly, not everyone wants to do the work that it takes to actually get there. And I don't mean that in a condescending way, because, really, who *would*? Not everyone wants to load amps and drum cases into a freezing back-alley bar at three in the afternoon and play for two kids plus the hungover sound guy, and understandably so. Not everyone wants to deal with the gut-wrenching humiliation and rejection involved in climbing your way up. People generally don't get excited over the idea of sleeping in a van and living on Taco Bell and Red Bulls for years on end. It's just not that fun after the novelty wears off.

So people change their minds. They decide to become accountants and truck drivers and secretaries—jobs that can give them health insurance and help them afford a mortgage—while also maybe playing some guitar with their friends on the side.

That's totally okay. It is all right to have wanted to be one thing with every shred of your soul and then later end up wanting a different thing and living a different life than you had imagined as a teenager. Part of loving yourself means listening to what your soul is saying to you *now*, not when you were six. It's okay to stop doing something that's too hard or makes you no money or just isn't fun anymore. A lot of my musician friends have stopped trying to be professional musicians and have gone on to lead different, happier lives instead.

Most of the time, trying to "make it" is too hard to be worth it. There's zero shame in that. Changing your mind isn't the same as giving up. I'm all about making a mature, smart decision and changing your mind if you want to. Our drummer Adam did that. He was thirty years old, sick of the grind and the poverty, and wanted to be a grown-up for once and have a normal marriage. He'd lived a decade as a crazy gigging musician, and now he was ready to move on. That's cool. Shawn and I weren't ready to do that. We still wanted to play the odds and live insane lives in exchange for sharing our music with people. It was still worth it to us, but it wasn't for Adam. Adam is a soulful and passionate person, and I'm confident he will find something else to pour himself into that will make him feel fulfilled.

One of our favorite video directors, Jamie Holt, attended one of the best film schools in the world. On the first day of classes, her professor made an inspiring speech that went something like, "Listen, guys. If you can see yourself doing *anything other than this*, I want you to walk out of this classroom immediately and go do that. This industry is awful. You will not make it. You will struggle the whole time and be broke. If you can think of any other profession as even slightly possible for you, please save yourself the trouble and go do that."

The day we met our manager, he opened up the conversation with, "This business is designed to ruin your life."

That's scary stuff.

For some people, though, it doesn't really matter. All the speeches in the world can't talk them out of their dream. Some people are so obsessed with their passion that they do not care how much it all sucks. They can stomach the pain and they welcome the sacrifices because they are one of those crazy people. I think most people that end up making it in really tough industries are like that. A little unhinged in all the right ways for a certain kind of success.

All of this is to say that, if you want what you want with an all-consuming passion that cannot be put aside, then I have complete and total confidence that you will most certainly be whatever you want to be. You will be one of the "lucky" ones who just keeps on going, even when all common sense says it's probably time to move on. The people who don't give up are the ones who make it. The people who realize that their passion is ruining their lives and is costing them everything are the ones who don't make it—which, again, is totally fine.

Full disclosure: It's just all about joy for me. Being a musician makes me happy; happier than a consistent schedule and stable income would. When it stops doing that, I will need to stop, too, or at least make adjustments until I'm happy again. So honor that part of you that wants to be great and that wants to share your message with the world for as long as it serves you. Whether or not you want to be an actual rockstar is not the point here; the point it that is costs a lot to be great, and sometimes we just don't really want it that bad to justify the cost. But. If you're reading this and it feels like your heart is on fire, then you probably are one of the crazy ones. Good for you. Go get it, babe.

~~~

I am a sunshine fiend. I drink it up. I get this from my mother, who is also addicted to sunshine. I always have infinitely better, easier days when the weather is nice, and I have to consciously tell myself that God or the world is not mad at the human race every time it's cloudy. In fact, sometimes I keep my blinds shut in the morning, because I know it's probably cloudy outside and I don't want to deal with it. I'd rather live in a dark and gloomy house all morning than see the dark and gloominess from the outside staring back at me.

You can imagine, then, what a fool I feel like whenever I finally get the courage to open the blinds and sometimes it's actually a beautiful day outside. It's equal parts relief and embarrassment.

I notice that I sometimes take this "keep the blinds drawn" approach to other areas of my life, as well. Things like, "I'm not even going to talk to them because I know I'm not on their level," or, "It'd be pointless to try that because I'm not ready yet and can't really give it my best." It's a defense mechanism. It's a reject-them-before-they-reject-me approach, and it's small-minded living.

Admittedly, sometimes it's nice to have a few things on the back burner that, you know, *could* be really great, but they haven't gotten there because you haven't found the time to really focus on them yet. It's comforting to think, "Man, I bet if I really gave this my best shot, it'd be something amazing," when you know you're only currently giving 50%.

While it's comfortable to half-ass things, it's much more daring to really go for something. To declare to the universe, your family, and all your Twitter followers that something wonderful is coming. "Get your hopes up, world! Because I'm about to blow your mind!" But we don't like to operate like that, do we? We publish our website quietly to test the waters and see how it goes. We set up a booth at the local craft festival, but don't invite any of our friends. *I don't want anybody feeling bad for me if it doesn't do well.*

Stop playing small. Stop holding back! You've got something really, really good brewing inside you, and it's been put there with the expectation that it will be shared. Open the blinds—it's gorgeous out if you'd only look.

I find myself holding back in other ways, too. I don't know about you, but sometimes I feel as if I want to pace myself, like I shouldn't spend all my creativity in one place. I'll be writing a record and I'll find myself wondering if I should save a few of my ideas for the next record, like I'm scared that I'll run out of fresh inspiration if I use it all up now.

Don't hold onto your cards. Play the whole deck when the time is right. Don't hold back any of what you've got, thinking you'll need to save some for later. You won't run out. Like joy, creativity isn't a finite resource. Honor what your soul is telling you to offer the world today, and when you need more offerings, they will be waiting for you tomorrow. To hold back is to believe that your brilliance is finite; that there is a limited amount of light you can share.

Dare to dream for more, and then dare to ask for more. There's more than enough with your name on it. There's more than enough success, brilliance, and beauty for you.

~~~

Since I grew up certain that I would be a superstar (probably by the age of 17), by the time I met the guys in my band when I was 18, I was already a little panicky, worried that I was a full year behind in my dream. I kept at my musical passion, though, and together we slowly, steadily carved out Icon's place in the music industry.

The years passed, and kept passing, and every few months I would wonder why we weren't huge yet. Sure, I was doing what I loved, but not at the scale I'd always planned on. Who dreams of being in a mid-level band? It was tempting to internalize that, and sometimes that old self-flagellating victim mentality would creep in. I just knew I was destined for world domination, for *impact*, and I felt as though I could not rest until we were selling out arenas. Like, yesterday.

That didn't happen. It was a hard, painful pill to swallow, but I had to deal with it. I couldn't live in the past the rest of my life, bitterly wondering why I wasn't on the cover of *Rolling Stone* yet. My soul refused to let me stay stuck there, and I found that I had to keep evolving and finding joy anyway.

It finally occurred to me that, despite the lack of instant success, I had a lot of wonderful things going for me in its place. A happy, thriving relationship, for one thing. Albums that I'm proud of, a kickass podcast, my own clothing line, an enviable touring schedule, and a wholehearted connection with our fans. But most importantly, I realized that I have a happy, content soul. A sane mind. A calm spirit. These were things I thought I'd never find, but figured that if I did, it would only be after having gotten mega-rich and untouchably successful.

To tell the whole truth, the closer I get to reaching the dream I made for myself as a kid, the more I find myself grateful that it didn't unfold in the way I'd assumed it would. And, sure, sometimes I feel a little phony, like the runner-up in a pageant claiming, "I totally wanted to get second place! This is everything I've ever worked for!" But the closer I get to my own soul, the happier I genuinely am with the life I have. As a lot of successful people will tell you, most of the image that's projected to the public eye is a mirage. As I've come to see all of the messed-up parts of the music industry for what they are, I've become more grateful for where I'm at. I want to keep growing, yes, but never at the expense of my heart.

Switching dreams is a killer. Mid-course corrections are often humbling, painful, and intense things to go through. It's easy to revert to thinking "I guess I wasn't good enough for this. I guess people like me never get what they want." It's easy to fall back into the self-hate vortex and compare your progress to other people who seem to not be working as hard as you, or want it as much as you do.

In those moments, I believe life is trying to teach us something. Despite our best efforts, things didn't turn out the way we'd hoped they would. We learn that we can't control all of life's mysteries and twists and turns, and that that's okay. If we know how to meet this news with an open heart, it makes us kinder, gentler, and lets us move forward with a healthy awe at our place in the universe.

These days, I don't find myself craving mega-stardom like I used to. Wanting what I have means feeling really, really good about all the magic that's buzzing in my life right now, and not bitterly demanding that life give me a refund just because I didn't end up where I thought I would. It took a while for my feelings to catch up with my reality and to be excited about all the amazing things that our unique journey has afforded me. But here's the thing: *everything I had hoped being super-successful would give me, I already have.* Those feelings of love, validation, self-expression—I feel those on a daily basis, because my life is made up of those things.

I gotta say that I am honored that I get to impact people with the music we make, but I'm so glad it doesn't stop there. I'm glad *I* didn't stop there. It turns out that being a musician is approximately one half of what I want to spend my life on, and I'm loving the other half of my interests that our slow, steady growth has allowed me to discover.

So yeah, I "failed." I totally failed at having the influence I dreamed about from age three up. But you know what? I totally *do* have the life I wanted—parts of it just look different from what I expected. Also, I am totally succeeding at being the kind of person that I presently am happy to be, and it would be so silly for me to negate that just because I'm not living the exact life I had predicted I would be several years back. I make peace with my life, and with myself, every day. And peace with yourself is priceless.

When failure was never an option for you, and you failed, don't let that shut down your dreaming heart. Let your dreams evolve! Don't work your whole life towards something you don't even want anymore. At that point, whose dream are you serving?

You are constantly growing, so your dreams very naturally will grow and change, too. This doesn't make you weak, small, fickle, or overly emotional; it makes you healthy and ahead of your own curve.

Life is a dance, and when we resist its rhythms, we stop moving, stumble, and fall. Our lives stall, and we wonder why we feel frustrated and why we're not going anywhere. But I don't think life was meant to be lived that way. The music is playing, so get off your hot ass and dance to it.

~~~

Recently, I was flipping through YouTube channels and accidentally found myself watching one of the Kardashian sisters giving an interview. I make a point to say, "one of the Kardashians" because I am more than a little proud of the fact that I cannot identify any of them by name. The fact that I have not memorized which girl gets which name that starts with K means they haven't gotten me yet.

Anyway, I'm watching this thing for a minute, which is one minute longer than I'd intended, and soon I found myself thinking, *Hmm, she actually seems pretty sweet. She's really pretty, too. Maybe these people aren't so bad. Maybe I'm the jerk for assuming they're everything that's screwed up with society.*

So I stayed with the interview a bit longer, and before I knew it I was thinking, *This family has it made! They are, like, the most famous and successful people in the world. Maybe making a sex tape and exploiting your personal life is the key to success and lasting fulfillment!*

...Okay, not quite. But I did sort of secretly envy them for a minute.

Fame is a funny thing. It makes precious stuff seem worthless and disposable stuff seem important. Following my close call of almost modeling my life plan after a Kardashian, I wrote myself this little note, and I'd like to share it with you:

ACCEPTING YOURSELF AND YOUR LIFE

November 21, 2016

You would be wise to always prioritize your own happiness above your pursuit of success. Even if you want to be successful so you can impact more people with your art, even if your motives are pure and altruistic, don't forget this principle: If your happiness suffers for your growth and achievement, it is not real growth at all.

Defining "success" without regard for your personal happiness is madness. When your pursuit of fame or money or influence crosses over from fun and enjoyable into intense striving that leads to desperation, then your soul is the very next thing to go. And what would your art be then, without your soul? We must decide young, when our hearts are still soft, that we'd rather be happy than famous.

And if you have constructed your idea of happiness around being famous or successful, then this is a fast route to feeling like a failure. Your success is in the hands of others, not only your own. Why hitch your happiness wagon to an outcome that you cannot guarantee? It would be much better to learn how to find happiness from within yourself and in the people and beautiful gifts that are already in your life.

One more thing about success. Don't build your identity around it. If you do that, your self-worth will rise and fall based on other people's spotty measurements of you. It is a powerless and miserable way to live. You are an artist, you belong here, and you have something to teach us. Sometimes we get it, sometimes we don't. You may not always be fully appreciated or recognized for the unique offerings you bring to the table, but don't let that discourage you. Keep creating, keep showing up, keep joyfully bringing your work into the world.

When you were little, what did you want to be more than anything when you grew up?

_____

_____

_____

_____

_____

_____

What are some of your dreams now?

_____

_____

_____

_____

_____

_____

_____

What are you happiest about in your life right now?

_____

_____

_____

_____

_____

_____

Can you see any similarities between your dreams then, your dreams now, and the ways you currently appreciate and cultivate happiness in your life today?

_____

_____

_____

_____

_____

_____

215

CHAPTER 16

SURVIVAL SKILLS (BECAUSE LIFE STILL SUCKS SOMETIMES)

I work really freaking hard to be happy and love myself, but life still sucks sometimes.

It's not fair. Sometimes all my efforts seem to amount to nothing, and I feel like I haven't really come that far at all.

I recently did an online video event with our fans where I chatted with them about living a full life and took their questions, and overall it was just so very wonderful. I closed the session feeling buzzing and lit up, like I do while running off the stage after an exhausting, rewarding live show.

Shortly thereafter, I was contacted by someone close to me who was concerned about something I'd said during the video chat thing. I had mentioned that I used to bawl my eyes out on the floor all the time, you know, just mourning being alive and all, and he'd reached out to ask me about it. He was worried about me; he wished he could have been there for me. I thanked him for his concern, explained that he didn't need to feel bad, and that was that.

But I couldn't stop thinking about it. Because, really now, is this actually news for any of us? This whole "I bawl my eyes out about life on a regular basis" thing—this is not an anomaly, correct? Aren't we all just kind of sad a lot of the time? I don't mean these questions to sound cute or trite. It's just that my experience is that a whole freaking lot of us feel the hurt of being alive for a good portion of our lives—especially a lot of artistically inclined people. I think it's part of the packaged deal of being human. In fact, I am a little suspicious about anyone who doesn't feel sad for a healthy chunk of the time, or at least every once in a while. Maybe not bawling-on-the-floor sad, but, you know, feeling things.

I think there's a difference between feeling things deeply—including the hurt and the conflict and the confusion—and letting our feelings stop us from living full lives. I don't think I have clinical depression. What I do think is that I am showing up for life day after day, even though most of the time it hurts.

I don't want this to be discouraging or melodramatic. I have no intention of living in perpetual heartache or throwing my hands up and saying, "I guess this is just the way it is." What I'm really trying to do is make peace with this idea of being happy and hurting simultaneously. As you know, I believe in happiness, in joy. I believe I can go several days in a row feeling pretty darn terrific, as I have actually done this once or twice. I put a whole lot of energy into choosing joy. I believe life wants me to be happy and is eager to support me in this. But I still feel hurt just as often—if not even more—as I feel joy, so I just sometimes have to conclude that being alive hurts. I'm not doing it wrong; life's just painful like that. Happiness isn't some state that you reach if you work hard enough at it. It's an ever-fluctuating journey of living one's life, and life often includes a heck of a lot of struggle, confusion, and pain.

I think most of us are sad and lonely a lot more than we let on. For me, just knowing this is the case can help take the guilt out of being sad and help me chill out long enough to catch my breath, recenter, and maybe help me feel a little better.

~~~

All that being said, I'm in no way Zen or evolved enough to do fancy things like "sit with the pain" or "trust the universe" when my world is crashing down. When life is coming at me hard, I turn to go-to techniques like "curse life and cry" and "eat ice cream."

These things have their place. You need to treat your fragile heart gently, and when that thing is begging for a donut, it's okay to give in.

But I'm guessing that's not really the same thing as loving yourself through your pain. It's more like placating yourself. It's like sticking a pacifier in a baby's mouth to make it shut up. Real action inspired by genuine love is ideally both comforting and *helpful*.

Here are some ideas that I use to get me through.

MAPMAKING

When I am in deep pain, the most helpful technique I've got is mapmaking. Mapmaking has seen me through some pretty tough times, and I'd like to teach you how it works. Also, you should know that when I say "technique," it's really just something I made up, but it's been invaluable to me nonetheless. It goes a little like this:

When I'm in the depths of despair, I take a two-minute break to ask myself what's going on and I scribble it down real quick. It'll be something like, "Oh my God, I'm so effing messed up right now and stressing about the tour. I'm trying to be this powerful entrepreneur rockstar and I can't handle it and some punk said something really mean on Twitter yesterday and I just freaking hate it all right now." It usually comes out in one rambling, emotional vent session, but I know I can use it later. I just get the stuff out, and then go back to my pity party.

A few days later, I'm probably feeling fine again, because that's how I work. I think back on my recent episode with a wince and think, "Gosh, what was my problem?"

Aha! I know *exactly* what my problem was, because I was a good little student and *wrote it all down*! I pull out my notes, and in this more clearheaded space, I can look for clues. I can review my notes and see that I'm letting the overwhelm of the upcoming tour drain me. I'm taking people's hate on social media personally. Hmm, okay.

Now, was it really those two things that caused me to get all crazy and sad? Probably not, but when I was feeling down, I didn't know any better so I just blamed it on that. Still, it helps me to know what I thought the problem was in the moment.

From these notes, I can learn some other helpful stuff. Like, I see that I have a lot on my plate right now and am extra emotional about the touring stuff. Why am I feeling overwhelmed about that? Is there something I can do to take the pressure off? Is there a different way to see this situation?

I guess all that stress is making me extra sensitive. I might want to stay off of online social platforms for a bit until I feel a little stronger. I can also focus on all the sources of love and support streaming into my life from my family, my friends, and from loving notes I've saved from our fans.

Honestly, just this intel alone is really eye-opening. But the most useful part of mapmaking goes in reverse: When I'm feeling *amazing*, I do the same thing. I take a minute to write down what is contributing to this high. I'm trying to pin it down so I can recreate it for later when I need it most. Maybe I'll write something like, "Oh my gosh, I love being myself! I feel so artistic and creative today and have been sewing so many beautiful pieces. My home is so clean and open and I am calm and centered. Yum."

After I've written these things down, I'm free to ride out the rest of my happy wave in peace. Then, sure enough, in a couple of days I'll have another emotional breakdown. So, again, I can revisit my notes and turn them into a map.

Hmm, it looks like sewing really made me feel alive that day. Okay, sewing is a way back to my soul. Got it. Ah, and having a pretty, clean home really put me over the edge on the happiness scale. I guess my space is even more important to me than I thought.

The next time I start to feel a little numb, a little off, I can attempt to derail my breakdown by going into my sewing studio and feeling centered by creating something. I can make the effort to tidy up my home so I feel like my environment supports me.

And when I *do* end up freaking out past the point of no return, when I feel empty and hopeless again, I at least sort of know what to do. I can logically recall my past antidotes and get to work on them. Take a walk. Journal. Play piano. Tidy up. I've got these things embedded into my brain, so even when I'm in Crazy Mode, I can mindlessly follow my own previously laid-out directions to lead myself back to, well, me.

JOURNALING

It would be a crime to talk about survival tools without discussing the brilliance of journaling in a bit more depth. By now, you know I'm a total journaling addict. I can't imagine my life, or myself, without it. It helps me slow down the days and to mark a moment in time that I can then revisit later if I choose. The act of pausing and recording where I'm at at any given time helps me objectively see how I'm growing and where I'm at in my journey. We should call it journey-aling, because that's exactly what it is. Sometimes, I look back on old entries and feel like a proud mama, marveling at how far I've come. Other times, I read passages and feel bummed that something I struggled with a few years back is still totally affecting me today.

One of my favorite ways to use journaling is for time travel. I write myself letters on a regular basis to make sure that the person I'm becoming is somebody I'm actually cool with being. I've always been sort of terrified of slowly changing into a dulled-out, numb, soulless human being without even noticing it's happening to me, so I've made it a point to capture my true heart to serve as a reference at a later date. It was important to journal out my intense feelings as a teenager because I never wanted to forget their existence. I never wanted to become a parent and be dismissive of my kids' struggles, like so many adults grow up to do. Journaling also helped me feel like it would be okay for me to grow up and try to be happy without being as scared of losing my true self. If I ever got all weird and became some creepy, overly peppy, plastic person or, alternately, a shuffling zombie of a human being one day, at least I could refer to who I used to be and find my way back.

I also time travel by making emotional, desperate promises to myself, like how I will *never let myself get like that lady I met who lets her man stomp all over her* or *never act like that dude we toured with who has everything but is an asshole to his fans.* I also journal out my dreams for the near future and revisit them a few months down the line to see if I'm still on track—and whether accomplishing them actually made me any happier.

My journals act like my second brain, keeping me sane and calm. They're my smart, objective, big-picture authority figure with twenty-twenty hindsight vision. My actual brain hasn't always felt like my ally; to help with this, I've made self-study a focus, and journaling helps me do that. Exploring and writing down my feelings has helped me figure myself out, and now I find it easier to work with my brain. I can track the changes in my thought patterns and beliefs, and make sure that I'm okay with the person I'm becoming.

There are a lot of different ways to journal, and it helps to find one that's going to be supportive to you and be something you enjoy doing. I used to handwrite everything because of the self-expression it allowed, but a few years ago I switched to typing things out, which has several benefits. For one, I type much faster than I write, so I can get it all out at once; plus, I can actually read it, which can't always be said for my real handwriting. I also like that I can store it on multiple hard drives/cloud storage spots, so even if a fire or flood happened, my stuff would be preserved. I use a journaling software now, and I love how pretty and organized it all is. I can look over years' worth of entries and see all the different countries I wrote them in, what the weather was like, and search to see what was going on in my life at a specific time.

I also like video journaling, where I just turn my webcam on and go. This is great for people who struggle with the writing aspect, and you can learn a lot about yourself by watching yourself speak. I don't love it quite as much as actual journaling, but it's great for when I have a lot to say and don't want to think too hard.

Journaling helps me sort through everything and take an honest look at my fears. It makes it easy to dissect a situation and see what's really going on. I also really like to write myself letters, and I kind of act as my own therapist. I start by just bitching about a situation that's bothering me. I get it all out and go for as long as I want, pouting and complaining, detailing everything that's wrong. No editing, no judgment, and I make sure I'm really saying how I feel. Then I take a break to get my mind off it for a minute. After that, I like to come back, read my bitch-fest with a clear mind, and objectively give myself some kickass advice, which usually includes Smart Me telling Pouty Me to grow up a little and also trains me to see the brighter side of things. It's cheaper than therapy and much more entertaining to revisit later.

When we have a really hard tour booked, I write myself little love letters on pretty cards. I'll make half a dozen cards for the upcoming tour that focus on different issues I suspect I'll probably have. I seal them up in their respective pink envelopes and title them things like "For when you're tired and uninspired" or "For when you feel average." They're a delight to savor on the road and open as needed, and I line them up in my bunk after opening them. It might be a little strange, sure, but if it helps me feel supportive of my future self and draw comfort when I really need it, then I'm all about it.

I did notice a downside with all this journaling at one point in my life. When I was like 15, I mostly wrote about how shitty my life was and all the awful things my parents were doing and what a waste of a human being I was. It wasn't pretty. I noticed that sometimes I would skip a few weeks of journaling and come back with, "Sorry I haven't written in a while. There wasn't much to write about…everything's been all right lately." I realized how cyclical it was for me; I would feed my own sadness by spelling it out and giving it so much attention. When I stopped hyperfocusing on my pain, there seemed to be less pain to deal with. Even this was a lesson learned, eventually—I learned by looking back at these old entries to not let myself focus so hard on my sadness, since it doesn't end up bringing me anywhere good.

If you want to start or up your journaling game, a great place to begin is by deciding to make it a safe space for you to be and love yourself. Maybe pick up a pretty notebook and special pen and dedicate these items just for this new chapter in your life. Start the journal with a love letter to yourself that gushes about how fabulous you are, and promise yourself that no matter what happens or what drama fills the pages ahead, you are committed to honoring yourself and not using your journal as a means to beat yourself up.

A REALITY CHECK

Whenever I'm feeling overwhelmed in life, it helps me to know what I'm working with. I get into this habit of thinking that my current pace of life is an anomaly; soon everything will slow down and I will catch my breath and finally deal with all my internal issues. But here's the thing:

Life isn't gonna stop being crazy. Let's just settle that right there.

It's not gonna slow down for us so we can finally catch our collective breath and get caught up on everything we want to do in life. It's not gonna pause long enough for us to make a game plan and then start back up again when we give it the go-ahead, however awesome that would be. This being the case, we need to learn to make the non-stop rhythms of life work for us. We need to create space for breath and rest; we need to *make space for space*. This will make everything in your life flow better: your work, your relationships, your art, you name it.

It starts with observing and making peace with the realities you're currently working with. Take stock of how crazy your life is by giving it a bird's eye view. Look at it through a wide-angle lens and give the last few years of your life an honest, objective look. Were the last couple of years especially overwhelming because you were going to school and working a demanding job (or two)? Was last year especially tough because your significant other was going through a lot and you had to be there for them? Did you lose someone? Did you move?

Consider where you're going, too. Are the next few years gonna be especially busy as you make your mark on the world? Are you going to move forward in your dream career and get a new job? Are you gonna train for a marathon? Are you saving up for a home? Is having a kid a possibility?

It's so healthy to look over your life from a wider perspective and observe all the rhythms and patterns that your life naturally falls into. For me, I have two very contrasting, polar rhythms: Tour, and home. They couldn't be more different from each other, and the way I approach each season is tailored for each unique time. But the point is that I *know* that my life never falls into a steady, predictable rhythm, where I'm humming along and living my life and doing my thing. Just when I start to get into a comfortable groove with either being at home or on tour, my reality is jolted and I'm back at the exact opposite place.

This could be a disruptive, destructive way to live, but it isn't. My psychotic schedule actually serves me, because I've joyfully accepted that my life's rhythm is one of disruption. Chaos is my normal. I don't mean that as in "I lower my life standards to accept the crap," but it does involve accepting the realities that come with me doing what I want to do for a living. Once I acknowledge and accept my lifestyle, I am free to work within it and make it work for me. Instead of fighting the chaos, I dance with it.

It's profound.

Once we've made peace with our uniquely crazy lives, we get to take our rightful place as our own life's master and make our schedules work for us. In my own life, I let the constant rhythm of disruption play an active part in keeping me from getting stagnant. Every time I go on tour, I go into it with fresh vision and a new resolve to be content no matter where I am—sleeping on my van bench, dancing around on stage at a sold-out show, in a gross basement green room in Detroit, or exploring the streets of Prague on a day off. I approach tour time with excitement and expectancy, open to learn and grow and experience new things that I likely wouldn't in my native city. Every new place I visit, every new fan I meet, and every fast food cashier I interact with is a chance to build and add onto my life's palette of experiences.

Of course, after a couple months of that, my soul is equally inspired and drained, and I am definitely ready to spend some time at home soaking in my bathtub, giving my hair and skin a break from the products and traveling, letting my voice rest, and refocusing. (If you can hear the longing in my voice, it's because I'm writing this chapter while on the road. I'm in Melbourne right this second, and while happy to be here, I cannot wait for our upcoming two months at home.)

I always spend the last few days of a tour dreaming about my time at home. I often pinpoint a desire to get back to healthier eating, reconnect with friends, and make art by myself. I like to identify new areas where there is growth potential—could I be a little more "creative fairy wonderland" and a little less "business"? Have I kinda been neglecting my daily practices of intentional gratitude and starting my mornings mindfully? Usually. Home time after a tour is the perfect time to fall back into that rhythm, and to do so with more inspiration and enthusiasm than I would have had if I'd been home for six months straight. My crazy life keeps me on my toes and keeps my soul equal parts invigorated and restful. I love it.

What about you and your uniquely crazy life? Is there any clarity that comes to mind when you honestly take inventory of how "crazy" it is? Do you need to drop something that isn't working for you anymore? Have you been neglecting something you had intended to do a few months back, but life took over and you kinda forgot? Take calm, mindful inventory regularly, and then decide to make peace with whatever conditions you're working with. From that place, you're in the perfect position to make life-giving adjustments as the creator of your own destiny. Ask yourself:

Have I been feeling mostly drained, or mostly lit up lately?

Do I look forward to my day, or do I dread getting out of bed?

How often do I find myself daydreaming about a life different from the one I have?

Pay attention to your answers, because signs of dissatisfaction are actually here to serve you. They exist to tell your soul that something is off and to help guide you back into a healthy place. Listen to those signs and let them point you in the direction that you *do* want your life to go. The fact that your head or your body is complaining is a good sign, even if it doesn't feel that way in the moment; it means a part of you is healthy enough to detect that something's off, and that same awareness can help get you back on track.

It helps to keep your perspective instead of getting sucked in every time. When your life is crashing down on you, allow some logical part of your brain to remind you that this won't last forever. When you're feeling on top of the world, don't get delusional and think this will somehow never end. I used to get so frustrated by my dramatic ups and downs, but now I accept them as somewhat normal. I don't get upset with myself for getting knocked off-center; I just asses where I'm at and then lovingly *recenter*. No need to beat myself up or catastrophize the situation. Part of being alive is getting off-center. Part of a great life is regular recentering.

BRUTAL/BEAUTIFUL

It seems to me that, for much of my life, I've been asking the same question over and over and over. It's probably why I love journaling so much and why I analyze my feelings into the ground. I want to know, once and for all:

Is life inherently good?
Does life have a vested interest in our happiness?
Is the universe a good guy or a bad guy?

I really like it when I get to answer this question with a resounding *yes*. Yes, life is kind and God is good and all is well! It's sunny outside, see? I'm feeling great! I'm gonna be happy forever! I finally got this. I knew it—I *knew* life was meant to be freaking awesome.

And then, of course, *BAM*. The shit starts flying. A tragic school shooting or terrorist attack jolts me out of my rose-colored naivety. Or maybe it's a little closer to home, like news of a friend miscarrying or a soul-wrenching break-up. In those moments, I can say with certainty that life is shit. This is a joke. God doesn't care one bit about how we feel; he just wants us to endure life to prove our devotion. Things are getting worse. Best to shrivel up and quit while we're ahead and just admit we're all screwed.

I finally got tattoos after a decade of dreaming about them. Two: one on each forearm. The left says *brutal* and the right says *beautiful*. I took inspiration from Glennon Doyle Melton's book *Carry On, War-rior*[4], in which she discusses how life is both of these things, and you don't get one without the other. She calls it "brutiful," which is clever but not pretty enough to get tattooed.

I read that book when I was going through one of the hardest times I've ever lived through, and while my experience was shouting at me BRUTALBRUTALBRUTAL, I took comfort in hoping that BEAUTIFULBEAUTIFULBEAUTIFUL might make an appearance again in my life someday. So I went and got those words inked,

---

[4]Glennon Doyle Melton. *Carry On, Warrior: The Power of Embracing Your Messy, Beautiful Life.* New York: Scribner, 2014.

because they answer all my questions for me. They put an end to the confusion and riddling in my mind once and for all. Life is not an either/or situation. It's both.

While I was in the middle of the Super Shitty Time, I wrote the following in my journal one morning:

September 30, 2015

Last night Adam told me he is leaving the band. I am distraught over the news, and feel it comes at an especially difficult time. With Shawn still away in treatment, and a lot of things up in the air, it feels like one more piece thrown into the shit storm currently circulating over my life.

I couldn't sleep last night, my head would not stop talking. This morning I got up from a difficult night, headed into the living room, and did what I know to do. I made some coffee. I turned on some relaxing Native American flute music, which makes me feel tranquil and connected. I lit a candle. I prayed. "WTF, God? Please help me."

As I'm sitting on my couch trying to get all Zen and feel God, I have a hard time hearing my pretty spa music because today is mowing day. Outside my window are three different dudes in bright orange work shirts mowing and trimming and blowing. The sound comes and goes, overpowering the thoughts in my head. I try to sit still and be present, but the intense decibel of the mowers keeps taking over everything.

And I think, I can try to pretend these dudes aren't here. I can try to out-Zen them with my deep relaxing meditative state.

I am calm.

I am with God.

Dammit—could you get any closer to my window, buddy?!?

I think there are a lot of us who pretend life is somehow free of the metaphorical orange-shirt-mowing-shitstorm-makers. These people maybe get lucky for a few years and have it really good. They sit there in their Zen state, and if they are famous, they try to tell us what their "secret" is.

Wanna know what their secret is? It's not their mowing day.

That's why they can sit in the quiet and vibe with their candles and flute music. They make it look so easy, because it *is* easy—for them. "Guys, I've got it!" they exclaim. "Just sit on your couch any day, any time, be still, and you'll feel it! You need to really *listen* for the music! And if you're not hearing it, then you're doing it wrong." Um, right. The rest of us are over here, desperately trying to block out the sound of the chaos two inches away from our face, plus now we're also feeling guilty about not being able to be Zen about everything 24/7.

Mowing days happen to us all. Sometimes they're mowing months and even mowing years. There are times when you'll lose your Zen completely and you'll just have to hang onto yourself until the shitstorm passes. While this is happening, take care of yourself, and try to be grateful for what's working instead of focusing on what's not. Pray to God that tomorrow morning the grass will be short and the orange shirts nothing but a distant memory. You've weathered storms like these before, and you'll live to weather them again.

~~~

For the record, life is back to being generally beautiful right now. I am suspicious of it and unsure if it will last, but I'll take it. If I'm being honest with myself, I know that it won't last. Life will suck really hardcore again someday; maybe even later today.

Since getting the tattoos, I've been ceremoniously interacting with them whenever the beautiful or the brutal surfaces in my life. I had a magical day recently where appreciating all of life's simple pleasures came effortlessly and I felt eternal. I gently graced my thumb over the ink on my right arm and thanked life for being beautiful.

The next day, I heard the tragic news of a horrific tour bus crash that happened to some of our tour buddies. This was less than a week after the November 2015 Paris attacks, and I was struck with the ridiculous frailness of life and felt helpless in a world where it could all be gone in an instant. I was at a traffic light, and I took a second to kiss the word on my left arm in sacred acknowledgment that life was brutal in that moment.

I imagine that my life will be one long succession of feeling both of the extremes that being alive calls for. I don't get to pick one over the other. I must have both. This is a little disturbing, but not nearly as much as it is comforting. I don't have to wonder anymore, because I know the answer: It's all brutal, and it's all beautiful.

You don't have to be happy all of the time. Having bad days doesn't mean you're living your life wrong. You don't have to keep it together so people always feel inspired when they think of you or so that they never have to worry about you. You don't have to prove to yourself that you've finally conquered your personal demons and now you're just magically okay all the time. An inspired life means there's room for all of it.

We often forget this, and understandably so, because we keep getting the message that everyone else already has this stuff figured out. We don't often get see our heroes' breakdowns in real time, because they don't post about those on social media. We usually only learn about the addiction or the divorce or the suicide attempt after the fact, when they've survived it and are doing better than ever and are now on television to talk about how great their new life is. It can be very confusing and unhelpful. I understand why people don't want to, and shouldn't, share their most personal struggles with their audience as it's taking place. It's not especially helpful to broadcast your raw pain as it's happening and process it for the world to see.

But still, it's helpful to remember that it happens to all of us. All of us feel like losers some days. All of us feel hopeless and heartsick sometimes. All of us struggle with self-hate and self-doubt. The brutal stuff is what we signed up for, and it's the only way we get to the beautiful.

The way we get to the art.

CONCLUSION

I am backstage at a New York City theater, about to play a show with my best friend and partner in crime of almost a decade. Three years ago, I was in this same theater, throwing up my dinner in the downstairs green room. I was crippled with anxiety over performing for the big-shot booking agent who had come to see us. Apparently, he could make or break us, and our entire future depended on how we performed in the next 60 minutes.

We did all right.

He signed us.

This neither made nor broke us.

This time, there's no fancy industry guy in attendance—just a few hundred of my soulmates waiting to sing along with us. This time, all my anxiety is replaced with a buzzing anticipation, because I know what is about to go down in this room.

I take the stage without an ounce of fear—just lots of love and acceptance and fire.

I would say our fans healed me, but that wouldn't quite be true.

I guess I healed me.

Well, no—wrong again. I am still healing. I am being healed daily by my own hands, and by God's, and by all the support that life keeps offering to me.

Turning my pain into art is an intense and rewarding endeavor, and there is no end in sight. I am certain that the pain will keep coming for me, and keep not killing me, and I will keep screaming it out of my soul at the piano.

Usually this is a solo thing, but tonight we get to scream our pain out together. We get to love ourselves enough to feel all of it, and to transmute it into something else entirely. We get to take all our aliveness in our hands, and with it we get to make messy, magical, brilliant art.

I'll leave you with the same question I ask at the beginning of every Icon For Hire show, just so we're all on the same page and know what we're getting into. First comes pain, then comes art, and then—finally—comes the magic.

You ready?

ACKNOWLEDGEMENTS

Thanks to Mercedes for reading different variations of this thing approximately ten times.

To Shawn, for all your encouragement along the way.

For Jess, who pretty much taught me everything I know, which I have now taken and turned into a book.

Thanks to my family for letting me share my story without judgement.

Thanks to Sylvia Cottrell for making me sound smart and coherent.

And thanks to you, dear reader, for making it all the way to the end with me. I love you so.

JOURNAL
ENTRIES

Aug 17 - 2012

Tonight - a girl went on stage and smiled a big, bright smile, and she looked so calm + happy. ~~She~~ had electric energy, and she moved in a fresh way and looked like she was genuinely enjoying herself, like she understood what this moment was. She did not look like she had played the exact same songs the night before. She looked overcome by her surroundings. She did not give off the vibe that she was vain or spent too much time in front of the mirror - but she was beautiful. Captivating, the star of the stage.

~~calm + happy. She had electric energy, and~~
~~she moved in a fresh way and looked like~~

Aug 19, 12

Day one of loving my self was a smashing... success!
YES! All day long yesterday I tried to walk
slowly with my head up, to talk in that
purposed tone of voice, remain present, and
block out thoughts that were wrong. I got
frusterated about 30 min before we wnt
on stage because I had so much adrenaline and
my body felt nervous. That was the only time
i felt I did not have control. I was worried
I would not enjoy the show and my mind would
be attacked with panic and all the pressure
of the show with the cameras and all that.
→ But I ENJOYED THE SHOW! This is huge
for me! I have not "felt" like that on stage in
a long while. I kept remembering, "This is my time,
I will take it and enjoy it" and I'm so excited
that we have another show and I get to have
my moment of shining again today. This morning,
I found myself looking forward to the next show...
I am surprised that that rare. I di n't
just how unhealthy my insides had become.

Just to rant, it is incredible what a
difference liking yourself makes. It is incredible
how everyone else can tell me over and over
how much they like me - friends, fans, family - and
yet that does not make one bit of difference
in the inner dialogue. Oh one more thing

about yesterday - It was late evening and it
occurred to me that I was enjoying the whole
day! I was not miserable, notably unhappy,
waiting to leave. I have found myself so
unhappy lately - I was confused, because I
know my life is amazing - my home, my man,
clothes, body, band, creativity - and I did
not know why I was still kind of miserable.

Now as I realize how often I think
negative things about my looks, posture,
clothes, everything, it makes sense. When I
like myself, I like my surroundings. I feel
like I've found the secret of life. I will
do anything to hold on to this revelation.

unhappy lately - I was confused, because I
know my life is amazing - my home, my
clothes, body, creativity - and I did
not know why I was still kind of miserable.

Now as I realize how often I think
negative things about
clothes, everything, it makes sense. When I
like myself, I like my surroundings. I feel
like I've found the secret of life. I will
do anything to hold on to this revelation.

Jesus

~~[redacted]~~
~~[redacted]~~

I wasn't gonna write tonite, but this is my way of reminding myself i'm not ok. I wish i could get help. It's so hard, cuz i dont think i have too much crap, it's not so bad. Is it healthy to tell your self you're worse then you think you are? I wish i had a therapist. A christian one, who herd from God. Someone to tell me if i'm normal or not. And then tell me what to do. Cuz either way, i'm unsatisfied. Dude, am i expecting to much out of life? I wanna be a rockstar. kinda. WHERE DID MY DRIVE GO?!?

~~[redacted]~~
~~[redacted]~~
~~[redacted]~~
~~[redacted]~~
~~[redacted]~~

IMPERFECT
UNHAPPY

Will i eur be ok? When will i be able to stop rambling on? When will i be able to be myself? When will i feel safe enough to stop hiding? In 1,206 days 12 hundred days to much.

June 8, 03

[text redacted]

When things go wrong, on goes their music. And now, something is terribly wrong, and i can't listen. The ~~total~~ music, that i can handle. But the words... they hurt to much. Every line is like a fucking knife in my deepest core. This. Is. Wrong. They have done so very much for me, I wish this time I cant stop my life source. Damned either way though. I am disgusted w/ myself.

[text redacted]

I want to be a rockstar. Not surprising—
who doesn't, but if keeping real is my base,
becoming a rock star is my hope. I mean
life is crap a lot, and music keeps me alive,
it keeps allot us funktioning, if you can
call living second by second, breath by
breath funktioning. I just want to be able to
give back, you know? I am so very appreciative
of the words and beats that have kept me
stable each and every day. These incredibly
talented, unselfish people have stepped up
and have decided to be my suicide prevention.
Where would you be, without those beautiful,
unreachable Heroes?

So, ya, i wanna be a hero, too. I'm sure a part
of it is to make me happy + to feel like i'm
doing something right, good. But i honestly
think i just want to have people helped +

[Several lines of handwritten text are redacted with black bars]

I look around and i despise <u>EVERYTHING</u>. Myself especially. Even suicide doesn't exist. Nothing is not something. Something turns around and slaps me in the face. Something... is nothing. So then, how much worse will no thing be.

I don't deserve to breathe. Not suicidly though, don't worry your precious little head. You try to take the best of me. Go. away. <u>GOD</u>!!

~

I put on a happy face. Then i had non ore energy, so i stopped. + Everybody hated me for it. And as much as i want to please them, i don't have what it takes to fake again.

I'd pull the trigger but i don't have the strength.

[redacted]

→ You would be wise to always prioritize your own happiness above your pursuit of success. Even if you want to be successful so you can impact more ppl, even if your motives are pure and altruistic, don't forget this principle:
If your happiness suffers for your growth + achievement, it is not real growth at all.

Defining "success" without regard for your personal happiness is ~~madness~~ madness. When your pursuit of fame or $ or influence crosses over from fun and enjoyable into intense striving that leads to desperation, then your soul is the very next thing to go. And what would your art be then, without your soul? We must decide young, when our hearts are still soft, that we'd rather be happy than famous.

... And if you have constructed your idea of happiness around being famous or successful, then this is a fast route to feeling like a failure. Your success is in the hands of others, not only your own. Why hitch your happiness wagon to an outcome that you cannot guarantee? It would be much better to learn how to find happiness from within yourself and in the people and beautiful gifts that are already in your life.

One more thing about success. Don't build your identity around it. If you do that, your self-worth will rise and fall based on other people's spotty measurements of you. It's a powerless and miserable way to live. You are an artist, you belong here, and you have something to teach us. Sometimes we get it, sometimes we don't. You may not always be fully appreciated or recognized for the unique offerings you bring to the table, but don't let that discourage you. Keep creating. Keep showing up, keep joyfully bringing your work into the world.

Sep 30- 2015

Last night Adam told me he's leaving the band. I am distraught over the news, and feel it comes at an especially difficult time. With Shawn still away in treatment, and a lot of things up in the air, it feels like one more piece thrown into the shit storm currently circulating over my life.

I couldn't sleep last night, my head would not stop talking. This morning I got up from a difficult night, headed into the living room, and did what I know to do. I made some coffee. I turned on some relaxing Native American Flute music, which makes me feel tranquil and connected. I lit a candle. I prayed. "WTF, God? Please help me."

As I'm sitting on my couch trying to get all Zen and feel God, I have a hard time hearing my pretty spa music because today is mowing day. Outside my window are three different dudes in bright orange work shirts mowing + trimming + blowing. The sound comes and goes, overpowering the thoughts in my head. I try to sit still and be present, but the intense decibel of the mowers keeps taking over everything.

And I think, I can try to pretend these dudes aren't here. I can try to Out-Zen them with my deep relaxing meditative state.

I am calm.

I am with God.

Dammit - could you get any closer to my window, buddy?!?

NOTE FROM ARIEL

Hey love,

I really hope you enjoyed reading Turn Your Pain Into Art. As a special thank you for supporting my art through buying this book, I'd like to give you my "Self Love Daily Meditation," a thirteen minute audio download of affirmations and soulfulness to get your day started in the right direction. You can get it totally free at www.arielbloomer.com/freebie.

Stay fierce and brilliant and badass.... just like you are.

Love,
Ariel